IS DEMOCRACY
POSSIBLE HERE?

RONALD
DWORKIN

IS DEMOCRACY POSSIBLE HERE?

PRINCIPLES FOR A NEW POLITICAL DEBATE

PRINCETON UNIVERSITY PRESS   PRINCETON AND OXFORD

Copyright © 2006 by Ronald Dworkin

Published by Princeton University Press, 41 William Street, Princeton, New Jersey 08540

In the United Kingdom: Princeton University Press, 3 Market Place, Woodstock, Oxfordshire OX20 1SY

Requests for permission to reproduce material from this work should be sent to Permissions, Princeton University Press.

All Rights Reserved

ISBN-13: 978-0-691-12653-1

ISBN-10: 0-691-12653-4

Library of Congress Cataloging-in-Publication Data

Dworkin, R. M.
   Is democracy possible here? : principles for a new political debate / Ronald Dworkin.
      p.   cm.
   Includes bibliographical references and index.
   ISBN-13: 978-0-691-12653-1 (hardcover : alk. paper)
   ISBN-10: 0-691-12653-4 (hardcover : alk. paper)
   1. Political participation—United States.   2. Political culture—United States.
   3. United States—Politics and government—1989– .   4. Democracy—United
   States—Citizen participation.   5. Church and state—United States.
   6. Terrorism—United States.   7. Social justice—United States.   I. Title.
   JK1764.D88   2006
   320.973—dc22   2006012026

British Library Cataloging-in-Publication Data is available

The book has its origins in the 2005 Scribner Lectures, cosponsored by Princeton University Press and Princeton University.

This book has been composed in Sabon with Trajan Display

Printed on acid-free paper. ∞

pup.princeton.edu

Printed in the United States of America

10 9 8 7 6 5 4 3 2 1

For Raphael and Josephine Betsy

CONTENTS

ACKNOWLEDGMENTS

THIS BOOK IS based on the Scribner Lectures given at Princeton University under the auspices of Princeton University Press in the spring of 2005. I am grateful to the Press and the University for sponsoring the lectures and to the faculty and students of Princeton and others who attended the lectures and participated in the seminars that followed them. I am also grateful to my editors, Ian Malcolm and Patricia Williams, for much help.

PREFACE

I WROTE THIS BOOK during a period of special political danger for the United States, and my examples and quotations are drawn from that period. I write about political argument in the United States—or rather the lack of it—in the infancy of the twenty-first century. The book's topics, however, are much more durable and much less bound to the political culture of a single country than these examples and illustrations might suggest. Every economically advanced and culturally plural political society—including new democracies and seriously aspiring democracies—must find ways to choose among rival convictions about the nature and force of human rights, the role of religion in politics, the distribution of the community's economic wealth, and the character and forms of the politics through which those decisions are made. The book's topics are international and belong to no particular decade.

We need to find ways not merely to struggle against one another about these issues, as if politics were contact sports, but to argue about them from deeper principles of personal and political morality that we can all respect. I hope to find those principles and to describe them in a way that makes such argument possible even across what are now thought to be impassable political divides. I elaborate the principles by developing in their light a fresh formulation of the liberal tradition in American politics, a tradition that I believe has been misrepresented in recent decades by its opponents and, to some extent, by its defenders as well. Of course I hope to convince as many readers as I can of the appeal of that liberal formulation. But my more basic aim is to convince as many as possible of the rest that they have a case to answer, a case that they can and should try to answer if they wish to protect our best traditions of democracy as a partnership in self-government embracing us all.

I have written about several of the issues discussed here elsewhere, in a more academic and philosophical style, particularly about economic justice in my book *Sovereign Virtue: The Theory and Practice of Equality.* I have tried here to make my views on those issues—about the insurance approach to distributive justice, for example—more accessible to a general audience and more suitable for a role in general political argument. Many very important contemporary political issues are hardly mentioned in this book because they do not seem to me primarily to involve the particular principles of human dignity on which I focus. Americans do disagree about global warming, for example, and this may well prove to be among the most urgent and important problems we face. But the central issues in that debate are instrumental questions, not questions of justice or fairness, because the dangers we face are shared by all. I concentrate rather on issues on which people's apparent self-interest and personal commitments appear antagonistic, and the question arises whether they share even deeper interests and commitments that can shape an argument, not just fuel a war.

March 2006

IS DEMOCRACY
POSSIBLE HERE?

CHAPTER 1

COMMON GROUND

In Search of Argument

AMERICAN POLITICS are in an appalling state. We disagree, fiercely, about almost everything. We disagree about terror and security, social justice, religion in politics, who is fit to be a judge, and what democracy is. These are not civil disagreements: each side has no respect for the other. We are no longer partners in self-government; our politics are rather a form of war.

The 2004 presidential election was sickeningly divisive. Republicans said that a victory for the Democratic candidate would threaten the survival, even the salvation, of the nation. Vice President Cheney said that a victory for John Kerry would be a triumph for Osama bin Laden and America's other mortal enemies. Some Roman Catholic bishops declared that voting for Kerry would be a sin that any Catholic would have to confess the next day. Liberals declared the stakes just as high, but the dangers all in the other direction. They said that the Bush presidency had been the worst and most incompetent in our history, that its reckless wartime soak-the-poor tax cuts and horrendous budget deficits would damage the economy for decades, that the invasion of Iraq was an immoral, inhumane, and botched diversion that, so far from making us safer from terrorism, had immeasurably deepened our peril. They announced themselves not just disappointed but sickened by the election's results.

The vote was very close—decided by a relatively small number of votes in one state—and it was geographically clustered: the Republicans won the more rural Midwest, South, and Southwest, and the Democrats the urban centers, the coasts, and the industrial northern tier of states. The television networks colored Republican states red and Democratic ones blue on their electronic maps on election night, and the maps divided America into great, contiguous blocks of the two colors. Commentators said that the colors signaled a deep, schismatic rift in the nation as a whole: a division between incompatible all-embracing cultures. The red culture demands more religion in public life and the blue culture less. The blue culture wants a more equal distribution of America's wealth; it favors higher taxes on the rich and nearly rich. The red culture says that high taxes penalize the successful for their success and ruin the economy; it wants still lower taxes. The blue culture insists on less freedom for business and more freedom for sex; the red culture wants it the other way around. The blue culture declares global warming to be a grave threat and pleads for the protection of wilderness as a threatened irrecoverable treasure; the red culture believes it irrational to compromise economic prosperity to protect trees. The red culture holds that it is insane to limit in any way our government's power to fight our terrorist enemies; it is suspicious of international organizations and impatient with critics who cite the human rights of alleged terrorists. The blue culture agrees that terrorists present an unprecedented danger to the country, but it is anxious to nourish international law and support international organizations, and it is willing to run increased security risks rather than weaken the laws and traditions that protect people accused of crimes and threatened with terrible punishment.

Some commentators argue that we are more deeply and viscerally divided even than these political differences suggest; the stark political split emerges, they say, from an even deeper, less articulate contrast between two mutually contemptuous worlds of personality and self-image. Blue-culture Americans, they say, crave sophistication; they cultivate a taste for imported wine and dense newspapers, and their religious convictions, if they have any at all, are philosophical, attenuated, and ecumenical. Red-culture Americans guard a blunter authenticity; they drink beer, watch car racing on television, and prefer their religion simple, evangelical, and militant. Bush won the 2004 election, on this story, in spite of the fact that his first-term performance was unimpressive, because the red culture slightly outnumbers the blue culture at the moment and Bush managed to embrace not only the political preferences of that red culture but its morals and aesthetics as well.

It would be silly to deny that the political divisions among Americans are unusually deep and angry now and that these divisions run along a fault line that can usefully be described as separating a red from a blue political world. But the two-all-embracing-cultures story that is beginning to become received wisdom is at least an exaggeration. The geographic division of the 2004 election results does suggest that regional differences played an important part. But the two-cultures story claims more: that some deep general account of character or worldview runs through each of the two sets of political positions and attitudes, some deep account that forms each set into a unified culture of conviction, taste, and attitude. It is difficult to see what that unifying account might be. There seems no natural reason why people who favor more celebration of the Christian religion in their community's public life should also favor lower taxes for the very rich, for example, or why they should be less sensitive to violations of the human rights of accused terrorists, or why they should be more likely to resist regulations that might slow environmental pollution. I very much doubt that most of those who voted for Kerry prefer Chardonnay to Schlitz. Perhaps the two-cultures thesis is not so much an explanation of our politics as itself the creation of our politics. One dominant force in recent elections has been the political alliance between evangelical religion and powerful commercial interests, and that alliance seems less the result of an underlying, deep cultural identity than of a political masterstroke: persuading people who hate gay marriage that they should therefore also hate the progressive income tax.[1]

In any case, however, whether the two-cultures thesis reports a genuine and deep split between two zeitgeists competing for national dominance, as the commentators think, or whether it is only an amazingly successful political invention, that thesis now has a political life of its own. It has been seized on for polemical effect by both conservatives and liberals. Here is the version of the thesis offered by Newt Gingrich, the former and powerful Speaker of the House.

> Over the last four decades, America has been divided into these two camps. In the first are those elites who find it acceptable to drive God out of public life and who, in general, also scorn American history, support economic regulation over freedom and competition, favor a "sophisticated" foreign policy led by the United Nations, and agree with the New York Times. But Americans in the other camp who are proud of our history know how integral God is to understanding American exceptionalism, know how vital the creative and competitive spirit is to being American, and believe that America is worth defending even if it irritates foreigners who do not share our values.[2]

This absurd account of how Americans now divide is sadly not atypical in the hatred it declares for half our country. Many liberals are guilty of parallel absurdities: they paint most Bush voters as stupid or delusional or as terminally gullible peons at the mercy of manipulative and greedy plutocrats. The most serious consequence of the assumption of a comprehensive and unbridgeable cultural gap is not the stereotyping, however, or even the contempt each side shows for the other. It is the lack of any decent argument in American political life.

I mean "argument" in the old-fashioned sense in which people who share some common ground in very basic political principles debate about which concrete policies better reflect these shared principles. There was none of that kind of argument in the formal election rhetoric of the last presidential election—in the nominating convention oratory or the unending television commercials. The three presidential debates were hailed by some journalists as unusually revealing, but they were not. The rules of the debates, as usual, stifled sustained argument about any issue, and journalists reporting the debates wrote and talked almost entirely not about an argument but about the demeanor and body language of the candidates.

Formal campaign rhetoric has not been much to brag about in the United States for a very long time: perhaps since the Lincoln-Douglas debates. But the news is not much better when we look beyond the formal campaign to the contributions of public intellectuals and other commentators. Intellectuals on each side set out their own convictions, sometimes with great clarity and eloquence, and they described the allegedly radical inhumanity and danger of the other side's views. But neither side made any proper effort to find the common ground that makes genuine argument among people of mutual respect possible and healing.

Here is one example—I believe entirely representative—of the wholly unargumentative character of our politics now. Gay marriage was much discussed by the candidates and in the media and was, according to the exit polls, an issue of considerable importance for the public. Neither candidate would say a word for it; both agreed that true marriage is between a man and a woman, and they disagreed only about whether it is appropriate to forbid gay marriage through constitutional amendment, a prospect both candidates understood was probably impossible anyway. Still it became a political issue, and most of those who thought gay marriage an abomination apparently voted for Bush. But in spite of all the attention to the issue, neither candidate seemed even to notice, let alone reply to, the careful case made by Chief Justice Margaret Marshall of the Massachusetts Supreme Court that the widely shared principles of her state's constitution required her to decide that gay marriage be permitted no matter how offensive that might seem to most people. Her decision was treated simply as an event that might be capitalized on by one side and might embarrass the other, with no apparent concern about whether her claim that established principles required that decision was right. After all the shouting and denouncing, there can be only a tiny number of Americans who have any idea what the legal argument was about.

If the two-cultures view is right, the lack of argument in American politics is understandable and inevitable. The split between the two cultures would be an unbridgeable gulf separating the comprehensive and wholly clashing worldviews of two Americas. If that is so—if the division between the two cultures is not just deep but bottomless—then there is no common ground to be found and no genuine argument to be had. Politics can be only the kind of war it has become. Many students of our politics think that that is our situation, and they may be right. But that would be alarming and tragic. Democracy can be healthy with no serious political argument if there is nevertheless a broad consensus about what is to be done. It can be healthy even if there is no consensus if it does have a culture of argument. But it cannot remain healthy with deep and bitter divisions and no real argument, because it then becomes only a tyranny of numbers.

Is the depressing diagnosis right? Is there really no common ground to be found between the trenches of two hostile political armies? Is no real argument possible?

My Agenda

I pursue two projects in this book, and I distinguish them now because I hope that many readers will agree with me about the first even if they largely disagree with me when I begin on the second. I shall argue, first, that in spite of the popular opinion I just described, we actually can find shared principles of sufficient substance to make a national political debate possible and profitable. These are very abstract, indeed philosophical, principles about the value and the central responsibilities of a human life. I suppose not that every American would immediately accept these principles, but that enough Americans on both sides of the supposedly unbridgeable divide would accept them if they took sufficient care to understand them. I shall then try to show the force and bearing of those shared principles on the great issues that divide us: issues about human rights, the place of religion in public life, social justice, and the character and value of democracy. Because I am mainly concerned with American political life in this book, I shall for the most part speak of these principles as the common property of Americans, but of course they are shared by a great many other people in the world, particularly in those mature democracies that Americans take to be their nation's political siblings.

It would have been nice, or at least polemically useful, had I been able to report that my own conclusions in this second, substantive project split the difference between the supposed red and blue cultures, offering some conclusions favorable to the convictions of each side. But that is not the case; the political opinions that I believe follow from our shared principles will strike readers as in fact a very deep shade of blue. I do not mean that they are all traditional liberal opinions; indeed some of them will not seem familiar at all. Liberals have not yet succeeded in creating a contemporary statement of their basic principles and have therefore been unnecessarily on the defensive in recent elections. It is part of my purpose in this book to state a form of liberalism that is not simply negative but sets out a positive program firmly based in what I take to be common ground among Americans. The liberalism I offer is what, in my view, liberalism means and requires now.

It is not surprising that my convictions are all of the same political hue, however, and that does not throw doubt on my suggestion that I begin in principles that we all share. On the contrary; it rather shows how deep these shared principles are. They are sufficiently basic so that a liberal or conservative interpretation of them will ramify across the entire spectrum of political attitudes. I hope readers who disagree with me—these might well be most of them—will therefore take what I say as a challenge. If you accept the premises I am about to suggest, and you disagree with my more concrete political convictions, then you must satisfy yourself that you can interpret those premises in a way that shows why I am wrong. If you can, then we have a foundation for genuine political argument. We can argue about whether your or my interpretation of the shared premises is coherent and if both are, which is more successful.

I must show, of course, that we really can argue over these basic issues. I must show that there is enough substance in the deep principles about human value that I describe as common ground to sustain an argument about what follows, by way of social, foreign, or economic political policy, from those principles. I do not assume that many Americans—or people anywhere—can be drawn into that kind of philosophical argument about those deep values. Most people on each side of the division now seem persuaded that it is useless to try to argue with or even to understand the other side. Evangelical Christians, for example, are rarely tempted to argue with those they believe to be secular humanists and therefore stuck in irremediable error. My ambitions are more modest but still very high. I hope to persuade enough people that this popular opinion is wrong—that it is profitable to study our most heated political controversies at a more philosophical level—to help begin a process that might later reinvigorate the argumentative dimension of our politics.

I shall not describe in any detail the laws and institutional arrangements that my own interpretation of the basic principles we share would support, but I shall describe some of these in a general way as illustration. I shall propose, for example, in the course of the book, that our legal and military procedures of detention should permit no distinction between citizens and foreigners, that political commercials should be banned from television during the months before a national election, and that the very poor should be regarded, like a minority and disadvantaged race, as a class entitled to special constitutional protection. I will not speculate much about the political possibilities of realizing these and my other now unpopular suggestions. At least some of them are politically utopian—it would be nearly impossible to persuade a majority of Americans to accept them, at least for a long time to come—and some would require constitutional amendment. I am a lawyer, and I will say something, particularly in the last chapter, about constitutional law. But my main interest is in political principle, not law. Utopias have their uses; they can concentrate the mind on the real limits of what is possible. In any case, this is no time in the life of the nation—or for that matter in my own—for caution.

The Two Dimensions of Human Dignity

No doubt almost all Americans agree on certain fairly concrete political principles; we agree, for example, that it would be wrong to jail a newspaper editor just because he has criticized the government. But the common ground we need in order to sustain a genuine large-scale argument about what divides us cannot be found in principles of that level of concreteness. We must look much further back; we must look not to principles that are distinctly political or even moral but rather to principles that identify more abstract value in the human situation. I believe that almost all of us, in spite of our great and evident differences, share two very basic such principles. Each of these is more complex than might first appear, and I will elaborate each throughout the book in discussing its implications for political policy. But I should first state them in their most abstract form.

The first principle—which I shall call the principle of intrinsic value—holds that each human life has a special kind of objective value. It has value as potentiality; once a human life has begun, it matters how it goes. It is good when that life succeeds and its potential is realized and bad when it fails and its potential is wasted. This is a matter of objective, not merely subjective value; I mean that a human life's success or failure is not only important to the person whose life it is or only important if and because that is what he wants.[3] The success or failure of any human life is important in itself, something we all have *reason* to want or to deplore. We treat many other values as objective in that way. For example, we think we should all regret an injustice, wherever it occurs, as something bad in itself. So, according to the first principle, we should all regret a wasted life as something bad in itself, whether the life in question is our own or someone else's.

The second principle—the principle of personal responsibility—holds that each person has a special responsibility for realizing the success of his own life, a responsibility that includes exercising his judgment about what kind of life would be successful for him. He must not accept that anyone else has the right to dictate those personal values to him or impose them on him without his endorsement. He may defer to the judgments codified in a particular religious tradition or to those of religious leaders or texts or, indeed, of secular moral or ethical instructors. But that deference must be his own decision; it must reflect his own deeper judgment about how to acquit his sovereign responsibility for his own life.

These two principles—that every human life is of intrinsic potential value and that everyone has a responsibility for realizing that value in his own life—together define the basis and conditions of human dignity, and I shall therefore refer to them as principles or dimensions of dignity. The principles are individualistic in this formal sense: they attach value to and impose responsibility on individual people one by one. But they are not necessarily individualistic in any other sense. They do not suppose, just as abstract principles, that the success of a single person's life can be achieved or even conceived independently of the success of some community or tradition to which he belongs or that he exercises his responsibility to identify value for himself only if he rejects the values of his community or tradition. The two principles would not be eligible as common ground that all Americans share if they were individualistic in that different and more substantive sense.

These dimensions of dignity will strike you as reflecting two political values that have been important in Western political theory. The first principle seems an abstract invocation of the ideal of equality, and the second of liberty. I mention this now because it is often said, particularly by political philosophers, that equality and liberty are competing values that cannot always be satisfied simultaneously, so that a political community must choose which to sacrifice to the other and when. If that were true, then our two principles might also be expected to conflict with one another. I do not accept this supposed conflict between equality and liberty; I think instead that political communities must find an understanding of each of these virtues that shows them as compatible, indeed that shows each as an aspect of the other.[4] That is my ambition for the two principles of human dignity as well.

I make, as I said, two claims for these principles. I claim, first, that the principles are sufficiently deep and general so that they can supply common ground for Americans from both political cultures into which we now seem divided. I shall try to defend that claim in the remainder of this chapter by describing the principles in greater detail. I claim, second, that in spite of their depth and generality, these principles have enough substance so that we can sensibly distinguish and argue about their interpretation and consequences for political institutions and policies. That second claim is the burden of the rest of the book.

The Intrinsic Value of a Human Life

The first principle of human dignity, which insists on the intrinsic and objective importance of how a human life is lived, may seem too pious and noble to have the popularity I claim for it. I shall try to convince you that most people would accept it on reflection, however, by persuading you first that most people think it is intrinsically and objectively important how their own life is lived and then, second, that most people have no reason to think it is objectively any less important how anyone else's life is lived.

Start with yourself. Do you not think it important that you live your own life well, that you make something of it? Is it not a matter of satisfaction to you and even pride when you think you are doing a good job of living and a matter of remorse and even shame when you think you are doing badly? You may say that in fact you aim at nothing so pretentious as a good life, that you only want to live a decently long time and have fun so long as you live. But you must decide what you mean by that claim. You might mean, first, that a long life full of pleasure is the best kind of life you can live. In that case you actually do think it important to live well, though you have a peculiarly hedonistic conception of what living well means. Or you might mean, second, that indeed you do not care about the goodness of your life as a whole, that you want only pleasure now and in the future.

In fact almost no one takes the latter view. People who say that they want only pleasure out of life do not in fact want only as much pleasure as they can have right now or in the future. They also want their lives to have *been* full of pleasure. They regret pleasures missed or foregone; they complain that they should have had more sex or traveled more or had more of other kinds of fun in the past. It does not explain that kind of regret to say that such people want the present pleasure of memories of past pleasure. They can find such memories pleasant now only because the memories confirm that they have lived well in the past. Of course not many people have such a strongly hedonistic opinion about what living well means. Most people think that enjoyment is central to a good life but not the whole story, that relationships and achievements are also important to living well. But even people who do think that pleasure is the only thing that counts actually accept the first principle of dignity for themselves. They think it important that they lead lives that are successful on the whole, which is why they care about pleasure past as well as pleasure to come.

So most of us, from both of our supposedly divided political cultures, accept that it is important not just that we enjoy ourselves minute by minute but that we lead lives that are overall good lives to lead. Most of us also think that the standard of a good life is objective, not subjective in the following sense. We do not think that someone is doing a good job of living whenever he thinks he is; we believe that people can be mistaken about this transcendently important matter. Some people who think that a good life is just a life full of fun day by day later come to believe that this is an impoverished view of what it is to live well. They are converted to the more common view: that a satisfactory life must have some level of close personal relationships, or of important achievement of some sort, or a religious dimension, or greater variety, or something of that sort. Then they believe that they were wrong in the past. Much of our most arresting literature—Tolstoy's haunting story of Ivan Illytch, for example—is precisely about the special pain of that kind of discovery. Or, indeed, we can make the opposite discovery, or at least think we have. Some people lead what they take to be bleak lives of tedious industry and then suddenly take pride, later, in what they have done and how they have lived.[5]

It would be very hard—I think impossible—for most of us to give up the idea that there is an objective standard of success in living, that we can be mistaken about what living well means, and that it is a matter of great importance that we not make that mistake. If we abandoned that assumption, we would find it difficult to make any of the important decisions we now make out of our sense of what it is to create a successful life. We cannot make such decisions, for instance, just by trying to predict what we will enjoy, because whether we enjoy doing or having something depends too much on whether we think enjoying it is part of living well. True, some philosophers are skeptical about all objective value; they say our opinions about how to live are not reports of objective fact but just projections of our deepest emotions. This skeptical position is a philosophical confusion; I have tried to explain why elsewhere.[6] But even these skeptical philosophers suppose that there is a better and a worse way for them to live and that it is important to live in the better way. They prefer to describe this conviction not as a belief but as an emotional projection, but that does not alter the fundamental role the conviction nevertheless plays in their lives. Some skeptics may take to their beds and cease making decisions altogether. But most of them continue their lives as if they believed what the rest of us believe: we can make mistakes about what it is to live well, and these mistakes are matters for very great regret.

Most of us, again from both our supposed cultures, share a further relevant conviction: we think that the importance of our leading successful rather than wasted lives does not depend on our wanting to do so. We want to live good lives because we recognize the importance of doing so, not the other way around. Some things are indeed important to us only because we happen, heaven knows why, to want them. I wanted the Boston Red Sox to win a baseball championship in 2004; it surprised me how important that was to me. But it would be absurd for me to think that the Red Sox's success was a matter of *objective* importance, that I would have made a mistake *not* to treat it as important. Some people want to climb high mountains, to learn to play all the Mozart sonatas, even though only indifferently, or to collect all the postage stamps ever printed. These achievements matter enormously to them, they may dedicate their lives to them, and yet the achievements have no independent objective importance no matter how fervently they are sought. Someone's failure to achieve what he thinks so important does of course make his life worse. But this is only because he does think it important, only because that is what he wants. Having a successful life is not like that. Most of us think that people who do not care what their lives are like, who are only marking time to their graves, are not just different from us in the unimportant way that people are who happen not to care whether the Red Sox win. We think that people who do not care about the character of their lives are defective in a particular and demeaning way: they lack dignity.

Now I must raise a further question. If (as I now assume) you believe that it is of objective importance how you live, then what reason do you have for believing this? What further convictions might you have that explain and justify this belief? You began dying when you were born, and that dying will not take very long. Why should it matter what you make of your terribly brief life? If you believe that there is a god, and that you are committed to his or its purposes, then you might answer that it is important how you live because that god wants you to live in a certain way. But many of us must try to answer that question without that hypothesis, which means that we must try to find something else beyond a supernatural being whose desires can explain the importance of how we live. I do not think we can do that. It will not serve to cite some cause we take to be supremely important like the power or flourishing of some nation or ethnic group or even of the human race. The importance of such a cause explains why we should care very much that it flourish, but it does not explain why it is important, for each of us, that it be he who has contributed to its flourishing. If you do not believe in a religious foundation for life's importance, then you must say that the importance of your having a good life is axiomatic and fundamental. It is important for no further reason than that you have a life to live.

In either case, whether you think the importance of your leading a good life depends on a god's wish or whether you think that that importance is axiomatic, the second issue I distinguished a few paragraphs ago arises. Is there anything about you that could make it a matter of greater objective or cosmic importance how your life goes than how mine goes or anyone else's? In times past many people have thought that their god cared more about them or their sect than about people in general, and they could therefore consistently claim that their lives mattered but that the lives of people in general did not. Millions of people apparently still believe that; many of them think that their god wants them to kill those who do not embrace the true faith. But I do not think that even Americans who would call themselves evangelists or fundamentalists think that the god they worship cares only or even mainly for them. Our American religions are religions of humanity; they teach that there is one god who treats all people as his children and has equal concern for them all. Very few Americans would admit to claiming a theological basis for any form of personal exceptionalism.

Nor could many of us openly claim any other basis for such exceptionalism. Some of the descendants of Richard Plantagenet or of the *Mayflower* passengers may favor the company of those they consider of equal pedigree, and unfortunately many people are racists who do not want to find blacks or other minorities in their neighborhoods. These tastes, however popular, have been classified as publicly shameful, and almost no one would openly admit to them. In any case, however, these relics of social superiority and prejudice are not germane now. They are tastes about association, not grounds for an objective judgment about the relative intrinsic importance of different human lives.

If, like almost all Americans, you do not believe that there is anything about you that makes the success of your life particularly important objectively, then on reflection you must admit to embracing the first principle of human dignity. You must accept that it is objectively important that once any human life has begun, that life go well and not be wasted. You must also accept that this is equally important for each person because you have no ground for distinctions of degree any more than for flat exclusions. This step that I ask you to take, from first-person concern with the success of your own life to a recognition of the equal objective importance of all human lives, has of course very important moral and political consequences. But I want just now to emphasize something different: the implications of the step not for your moral responsibilities but for your self-respect.

I suggested just now that you, along with most people, suppose that those who lack a proper appreciation of the importance of leading a good life lack personal dignity. They do not just happen to lack a taste that you have; they fail to appreciate something of objective value, which is the importance of their own life's being a success and not a failure. But if, as I am now supposing you think, that objective importance cannot be thought to belong to any human life without belonging equally to all, then it is impossible to separate self-respect from respect for the importance of the lives of others. You cannot act in a way that denies the intrinsic importance of any human life without an insult to your own dignity. That point is a familiar insight in moral philosophy. It is at the center of Immanuel Kant's claim that respect for our own humanity means respect for humanity as such; Kant insisted that if you treat others as mere means whose lives have no intrinsic importance, then you are despising your own life as well.

So it is crucial for you to decide when your actions do show contempt for the value of other people's lives. That is a question we shall pursue throughout the rest of this book. Its answer is far from obvious. It is a matter about which Americans may responsibly disagree, and, as I shall try to show, their disagreement about that fundamental question may help to explain how and why they disagree about more concrete political issues. It is also a matter about which Americans can responsibly argue.

Personal Responsibility for a Human Life

The second principle of human dignity I mentioned insists that each of us has a personal responsibility for the governance of his own life that includes the responsibility to make and execute ultimate decisions about what life would be a good one to lead. We may not subordinate ourselves to the will of other human beings in making those decisions; we must not accept the right of anyone else to force us to conform to a view of success that but for that coercion we would not choose. We must be careful to distinguish subordination so defined from a variety of ways in which others may influence us that do not involve subordination and that this principle of dignity therefore does not condemn. Others may give us advice, and we may be disposed, for one reason or another, to take that advice. We may admire and wish to imitate them in the values they embrace and the decisions they make. That admiration and imitation may be self-conscious, or it may be unreflective and even habitual.

The values and actions of other people may influence us in a more diffuse and reciprocal way: through their impact on the culture in which we all live. Critics sometimes accuse liberals of thinking that human beings can be self-contained atoms who decide questions of value entirely from within their own internal intellectual resources. It would of course be absurd to think this, and I know of no competent philosopher, liberal or not, who does. Culture is inescapable; few even wish to escape it. Much of American culture reflects the opinion that material wealth is a very important component of a good life, for example, and whether you agree with that judgment or not, your children will very likely be influenced by it in their choice of career and lifestyle. People are more likely to want wealth if wealth is offered as a symbol of success everywhere they look. None of these ways in which we are influenced by the values or actions of others constitute subordination to their will. But granting government or any other group the authority to require our adherence to a particular scheme of values on pain of punishment, or to dictate marriage partners or professions or occupations to us, would indeed mean subordination. That is what the second principle condemns.

Some Americans are individualists in the strong sense I mentioned earlier. They take pride in marching to the beat of their own drum, of following no one else's lead, of doing it their way. Others believe that it is an essential part of their living well to live within a particular religious, ethnic, or even familial tradition that sets a pattern of life for them that they feel no need to reexamine. They do not regard themselves as subordinated to the will of other people because they do not believe that anyone has coerced them into the opinion that this is the right way to live. They feel free to reexamine and revaluate that opinion if—however unlikely this might be—they one day find it appropriate. They think that they and no one else is still in charge of fundamental decisions about how they should live. They would be appalled by any suggestion that they should somehow put such a reexamination beyond their power by giving others the power to punish them if they ever, for example, took up a different faith. They think that agreeing to abandon their own continuing responsibility in that way would be inconsistent with their dignity.

Are any important religious groups or traditions in America unable to accept the second principle of dignity? If so, that principle could not figure as common ground among us. Some religions give special authority over doctrine to officials of the church hierarchy; Catholics, for example, accept a principle of papal infallibility on religious matters. But this authority is epistemic rather than coercive. The officials who enjoy it are understood to have special access to or knowledge of God's will, and a believer who accepts that special authority will therefore accept those officials' reports as true without question. That is not the kind of subordination that the principle of special responsibility condemns, because people who accept that epistemic authority have not thereby accepted that the officials to whom they defer have authority to compel deference through the exercise or threat of temporal sanction. They accept the religious authority and teaching of the church in the exercise of their own judgment that such deference is appropriate. It would be different if religious officials had the power to direct physical or financial punishment for those who refused to follow their instruction, as they once did in Europe and America and as they still do in many other regions. That kind of authority would indeed be incompatible with the principle of personal responsibility. But American religions believe, as a conservative religious scholar has put it, that coercing an act of faith against conviction does not merely "deprive apparently religious acts and choices of value as religious acts and choices: it prevents them from *being* religious acts and choices."[7]

Nor does the principle of personal responsibility forbid one to accept religious conviction or a religious way of life as a matter of faith or revelation. Personal responsibility does not mean scientism or even rationalism. A great many Americans believe that religious conviction is a direct gift from a god; they find confirmation of their conviction in spiritual moments and ask for no other kind of proof. But the faith they embrace in that way is nevertheless personal; it is not imposed on them by threat or brainwashing or other bludgeoning. Some religions do claim the power to impose faith in those ways, of course. Many cultures do not recognize personal responsibility as a demand of dignity, or they recognize it only for men and not for women, or only for religious or social elders or people of rank, and there are certainly representatives and vestiges of those cultures in America. But if, as I believe, these are only a very small minority of religious Americans, we may nevertheless claim the principle of personal responsibility as common ground fit for political argument in that country.

Once again none of us has any reason to think that he alone has that responsibility and that other human beings do not. There is nothing about any of us that could account for that difference; no religion with any traction in America supposes that only an elect should be free from subordination to the will of other people. We do think that some people are not capable of deciding important issues for themselves. But this is a matter of capacity, not status, and the capacity in question is basic rationality, not even normal skill. We do impose important decisions on children—about education, for example—even when they are basically rational, but we restrict these to decisions that they can in principle reexamine when they come of age. We do not deny basic freedom of choice in values to adults we think are basically rational, even if we think their judgment is very poor; we do not forbid even those we predict will make bad choices to marry whom they choose or read what they choose; we do not force them into jobs they do not want or assign them religious practices to which they do not subscribe.

However, I must now mention, though only to defer, a special problem that arises about the second principle of dignity. I said that this principle assigns each of us a personal responsibility for certain decisions about how to lead our lives. Which decisions? We can quickly agree on certain of these. We have a right and a responsibility to decide for ourselves about religion, marriage, and occupation, for instance. We can also quickly agree about decisions that people do *not* have a right to make for themselves. I cannot decide for myself what property is mine rather than yours, or whether I may injure you physically or imprison you, or even, as most of us now think, whether to wear a seat belt when I drive. The state makes those decisions for us all and properly coerces us to obey its decisions. The difference between these two kinds of decision is the difference between ethics and morality. Our ethical convictions define what we should count as a good life for ourselves; our moral principles define our obligations and responsibilities to other people. The principle of personal responsibility allows the state to force us to live in accordance with collective decisions of moral principle, but it forbids the state to dictate ethical convictions in that way. We shall see, in chapter 3, that this crucial distinction is more complex—and in detail more controversial—than this quick summary indicates. But the summary nevertheless states the essence of the distinction.

Common Ground and Controversy

I hope you are now at least tempted to agree that Americans across the political spectrum, with relatively few exceptions, would accept that they share the conception of human dignity that I have been describing. But that is possible only because different understandings are, at least initially, available about what follows by way of more political principles and policies from the two principles that define that conception. People are very likely to disagree about what follows about tax rates, for instance, from the principle that everyone's life is of equal intrinsic importance. I shall take up that question in chapter 4. They are very likely to disagree about what follows about abortion and gay marriage from the principle that people have a special responsibility for their own lives. That is one of the topics of chapter 3. More generally, people from what is called the red culture will probably be drawn to more restricted answers than those from the blue culture to questions about which actions show contempt for the value of other people's lives and also about which decisions must be left to individual conscience according to the right conception of personal responsibility. I must not suggest that only the particular political controversies I discuss in this book can properly be understood as disagreements about the best interpretation of the two principles. I have selected for discussion those disagreements that now seem most important, divisive, and intractable, but I might have selected others.

I have already warned that it would be silly to expect that Americans will cease to disagree radically about politics any time soon. It would nevertheless be a great improvement if they came to see their continuing disagreements as controversies about the best interpretation of fundamental values they all share rather than simply as confrontations between two divergent worldviews neither of which is comprehensible to the other. Citizens would then be encouraged to defend their concrete convictions about human rights or taxation or abortion by offering a particular and general interpretation of the shared principles that they believe supports those concrete positions. This would make a familiar form of argument possible: different parties of opinion might then try to show that the interpretations on which they rely capture more of the uncontroversial applications of the general principle than rival interpretations do. Or that these interpretations fit better with other values they might expect their argumentative opponents to share, or with facts they might expect them to recognize: social facts about the consequences of poverty, for instance, or biological facts of embryology. At the least, that different way of seeing our divisions could be expected to improve the respect in which each side held the other; each side could then see the other as a partner in trying to achieve goals they all shared and as contributing to that project by exploring strategies that others may not have fully considered.

That may seem an unforgivably unrealistic hope now. I have conceded that most people now have no interest in discussion or debate with those they regard as belonging to an entirely alien religious or political culture. It is realistic to hope only that a different view more congenial to argument can take root among a few people and then spread by examples of useful discussion that slowly diffuse the deadening two-unbridgeable-cultures attitude that we have been too ready to accept. I have not yet shown even that that beginning is possible, however, because it remains an open question whether there is enough substance in the areas of agreement I claim in order to sustain the kind of argument I just described. Do we commit ourselves to enough, just in agreeing that every human life has intrinsic potential value and that each person has a responsibility to identify and realize the potential value in his own life, to enable a genuine argument to begin? Or are these only empty slogans from which nothing of importance can be said to follow?

CHAPTER 2

TERRORISM AND HUMAN RIGHTS

Terrorism, Rights, and Security

THOUSANDS OF FANATICS around the world would be glad to die if they could kill Westerners—particularly Americans. They created an unbelievable catastrophe in September 2001, and they may already have weapons of apocalyptic murder that could dwarf the horror of that destruction. We are angry and we are also frightened. Information is our main defense; the more we know about the resources, identity, leaders, and plans of the terrorists the safer we are. One source of information is people: the people our military and police believe may be terrorists themselves or may at least have information about terrorists that would be useful to us. Americans disagree about what our government may do to those people to extract whatever information they have. Controversy has centered on three practices: surveillance, coercive interrogation, and indefinite detention.

Soon after September 11, 2001, Congress adopted a law authorizing new forms of surveillance so quickly that few senators or representatives had a chance even to read it. Though the law, called the USA Patriot Act, usefully allowed improved communication among federal agencies, it also allowed the government novel and—to liberals—frightening powers to invade privacy; it allowed it, for example, to conduct secret searches of people's homes without even informing them later that their homes had been searched, and to compel libraries to report the books people had borrowed. A coalition of Democrats and moderate Republicans forced the administration to eliminate some of the act's most objectionable provisions when Congress renewed it in 2006, but several of the new powers of surveillance that threaten individual privacy remain. In early 2006, the *New York Times* reported that President Bush had instituted an extensive program of secretly wiretapping both citizens and foreigners without securing the judicial warrants that federal statutes require. The president admitted the practice. He and his aides claimed that it was legal—among other grounds, because the president's constitutional power as commander in chief allows him to override the ordinary law—but few lawyers agreed.[1]

The Bush administration has not formally conceded that it has ordered the torture of suspected terrorists in American detention camps or "rendered" them to other countries for torture. But it is very widely assumed that it has done both, and the secretary of state, Condoleezza Rice, all but admitted this in response to criticism by European leaders after it was reported that the United States had established detention centers on their territories. The administration's Justice Department prepared and circulated memorandums arguing that the president has the legal power to order torture even though this is forbidden by law; the argument relies once again on the Constitution's declaration that the president is commander in chief. It is controversial, in any case, what constitutes torture; the administration apparently denies that certain terrifying practices, like repeatedly pouring water over a blindfolded prisoner's head to create the sensation that he is drowning, count as torture.

The United States now detains hundreds of prisoners indefinitely, without charge or trial, at Guantánamo and at other places around the world. The Bush administration says that these detainees are enemy combatants, but it will not try them or even inform them or the public of the evidence on which it draws that conclusion. We do not treat even the most dangerous of ordinary domestic criminals—those we suspect of serial murder or running drug rings, for instance—that way. Our Constitution forbids imprisoning such people just because they are dangerous or because they have information that would help us to prevent murder and other crimes. We have developed, over centuries, a jurisprudence of criminal justice that insists that the police must soon release people they have arrested but either will not or cannot prosecute. We also insist that those who are tried must be protected by procedures that so far as is practicable prevent unjust conviction. We say that it is better that a thousand guilty people go free than that one innocent person be punished. But the Bush administration has set aside all these constraints and protections on the ground that it can protect Americans more effectively against future terrorist attacks in that way.

All these policies of surveillance, coercive interrogation, and detention are novel, and they are admittedly extreme. They are all controversial, and the controversy in general, though not perfectly, tracks the liberal-conservative division we are now exploring. Many Americans approve of the administration's tough new policies. They say that our safety is now more gravely threatened than ever before and that we must, as it is often put, strike a new balance between security and freedom. Many other Americans disagree; they say that the new balance the administration has struck is too great a compromise of freedom, that the emergency is not grave enough to justify what the government has done and is still doing.

The controversy is partly about the best interpretation of American law and of the treaties America has signed and ratified. Some liberals argue that the more extreme provisions of the USA Patriot Act are unconstitutional, and most lawyers believe that the president acted illegally in ordering wiretaps with no judicial warrant. Many critics argue that the indefinite detention of suspected terrorists is unconstitutional because even foreigners have a constitutional right to the traditional procedures and protections that we guarantee to ordinary domestic criminals. In a very important decision in 2004, the Supreme Court held that the government had violated the Constitution by not allowing foreigners in Guantánamo Bay to contest their detention before proper tribunals.[2]

But the legal issue is not at the center of the disagreement because Bush's supporters think that the law is in any case anachronistic and should be changed. They say that the regime of constitutional and legal rights that American law has developed over centuries was made obsolete by the September 11 attack, that we need, in language I just mentioned, a new legal balance between security and the rights of an accused. So the real argument is a moral, not a legal, one.

The image of striking a new balance is popular, but it is also peculiarly inapt. It suggests that "we"—Americans in general—must decide what mixture of security and personal freedom we want for ourselves, in much the same way as we decide how elaborate a network of intercity roads we want once we know how much such roads cost and their impact on the countryside. The issues we actually face are very different, however, and the balancing metaphor obscures those issues. We must decide not where our own interest lies on balance but the very different question of what morality requires, even at the expense of our own interests, and we cannot answer that question by asking whether the benefits of our policy outweigh its costs to us.

Many conservatives believe that America is morally entitled to use untraditional weapons to combat an untraditional threat. They believe that the terrorists have forfeited any right to our concern by their barbarous actions and intentions and that the president has a duty and therefore a right to put American safety first and to do whatever he and his advisers think helpful to that end. In some part they rely on claims of fact that are false or dubious: they supported the war in Iraq, for example, because they accepted the president's claim that Iraq had a stockpile of terrible weapons, which they now know was not true, and also his claim that Iraq abetted the terrorist attack of 2001, which is equally false but which many of them still believe. But the deep dispute about America's antiterrorist policies is not centrally a disagreement about facts. It is about whether these policies violate human rights. If they do, they are indefensible even if they are legal and even if they do make Americans safer.

We use the concept of human rights to describe the most basic and universal of all rights; there is no more serious complaint against a government than that it has violated human rights. The United States and other nations invoke the idea to justify extreme sanctions; we refuse financial aid or economic advantage to countries that we accuse of human rights violations, and we try to stop other nations or agencies from helping them. We believe that in some circumstances we are justified even in invading those countries to prevent such violations. We cannot claim that human rights were made obsolete by September 11 because we believe such rights to be timeless. We cannot claim a privilege to disregard them when we believe our own security to be threatened because we insist that states must respect these rights no matter what reason they might have for violating them. So it is natural for the administration's critics to appeal to human rights when much of the public seems indifferent to legal rights.

We must be careful, however, to distinguish two somewhat different claims that critics make. Following the Second World War, a great number of nations entered into a variety of international treaties, charters, and covenants listing certain human rights and agreeing to respect those rights. These include, for example, the United Nations Declaration of Human Rights, the European Convention on Human Rights, and the Geneva Conventions that set out rules for the definition and treatment of prisoners of war. Some critics charge that America's treatment of accused terrorists violates its obligations under one or another of these treaties. There is a good deal of controversy among international lawyers about whether that charge is valid. The Bush administration argues, for example, that those prisoners it accuses of having fought for the Taliban or Al-Qaeda in Afghanistan are not entitled to the protections of the Geneva Conventions because they are "illegal combatants." A United States Court of Appeals has accepted that argument, but a great many leading international lawyers reject it, and I agree with them.[3]

This controversy about human rights is essentially a legal one because it turns on the correct interpretation of international treaties and other documents. Other critics make a different and more fundamental charge: that our detention policy violates what we might call true or genuine human rights, the rights that all human beings have just because they are human, the rights that the treaties should protect, the rights no nation should be permitted to violate even for reasons of security. The international treaties aimed to identify and protect these very basic human rights. But the treaties were inevitably compromises among different nations with different traditions and interests, and they are often criticized as failing to capture genuine human rights fully or accurately. Some nations and groups, particularly from the third world, believe that most of the treaties are defective because they neglect economic rights, for instance, and also because some of the alleged human rights they include are only parochial ideas recognized in the traditions of a few powerful Western nations, including (according to much third-world opinion) rights of free speech and of a free press. So even if the Bush administration were right in its legal opinion that the Geneva Conventions and other treaties technically do not apply to the Guantánamo detainees, the moral question would still remain whether our policies there and elsewhere do violate the detainees' underlying human rights, rights that the United States would act immorally, even if not illegally, in violating.

That second, moral question must be our question now. Americans apparently disagree sharply in the answer they give to it, and the disagreement seems to run at least roughly along the now-familiar red-blue lines. Liberals attack our detention and other antiterrorist policies, and conservatives defend them. This is one of the deep fissures that prompt critics to say that we are now a polarized nation. But though we disagree, we do not argue. There is no national debate about what human rights the detainees have, or even about what human rights are.

What Are Human Rights?

Politically conscious people use the concept of human rights freely; they use it, as I said, to make the gravest political accusations and to justify serious political sanctions, sometimes including war. But many of them would find it hard to say what a human right is. They not only disagree about what a proper list of human rights should contain—whether it should include economic rights or rights to free speech, for example—but find it difficult even to define a test for their claims, to provide an account of how we should decide which alleged rights do belong on such a list. These are important questions that require us to reflect more carefully about the very idea of a human right. If we are to make any progress in constructing a national debate about the morality of our antiterrorist policies, we must first confront that philosophical issue directly. Then, in the next section, we can return to the political controversies.

Legal and Political Rights. What are human rights? How do they differ from legal rights and less fundamental moral rights? We understand the idea of a legal right well enough. Government creates and enforces legal rights for a variety of reasons. A nation cannot have a functioning economy, for instance, unless its laws create and protect legal rights in property so that people can count on retaining what they earn in labor or trade. Some legal rights, which we call constitutional rights, have a special force and role: they prevent government from enacting laws or adopting policies that would otherwise seem attractive. The First Amendment to the United States Constitution creates legal rights of that kind; it gives citizens a right to speak that government may not abridge even when it would be in the general interest to do so. We often justify such constitutional rights by saying that people already have a moral right to what the Constitution makes into a legal right. The moral rights we have in mind are special because they are rights not against other people as individuals but against governments, and I shall therefore refer to these special moral rights as *political* rights.

Most legitimate acts of any government involve trade-offs of different people's interests; these acts benefit some citizens and disadvantage others in order to improve the community's well-being on the whole. When Congress stipulates a tariff on particular imports, a tax on particular luxuries, or a subsidy for farmers growing a particular crop, or when a state or city decides to build an airport, a sports stadium, or a new highway in one place rather than another, that decision helps some citizens and harms others. It is justified if its overall effect, taking account of the gains to some citizens and losses to others, is beneficial. If it really is best for everyone overall to build the airport near my house rather than yours, I have no legitimate complaint against that decision.

But certain interests of particular people are so important that it would be wrong—morally wrong—for the community to sacrifice those interests just to secure an overall benefit. Political rights mark off and protect these particularly important interests. A political right, we may say, is a *trump* over the kind of trade-off argument that normally justifies political action. The First Amendment gives Americans a legal right to be free from political censorship; we explain why that legal right is desirable by supposing that people have a political right to speak their mind that is sufficiently important to be protected legally in that way. (I consider some of the reasons why people are thought to have that political right in chapter 5.) The Constitution also gives Americans legal rights that guarantee them a fair trial if they are accused of a crime; we justify those legal rights by insisting that people already have a political right not to be jailed without a fair trial even if imprisonment would in some way benefit the community overall. We appeal to political rights not only to explain and justify legal rights in this way but also to criticize government for not adopting legal rights that we think it should adopt. Americans who think that affirmative action—giving members of minorities special preference in university admissions and in hiring—is wrong often appeal to a political right to justify their opposition. They say that majority students or job applicants have a right not to be put at a disadvantage in that way even if the community as a whole would benefit. Other people, who deny that affirmative action is unfair, say that there is no such political right.[4]

Someone who claims a political right makes a very strong claim: that government cannot properly do what might be in the community's overall best interests. He must show why the individual interests he cites are so important that they justify that strong claim. If we accept the two principles of human dignity that I described in the last chapter, we can look to those principles for that justification. We can insist that people have political rights to whatever protection is necessary to respect the equal importance of their lives and their sovereign responsibility to identify and create value in their own lives. We can insist, for example, on that ground, that people have a political right not to suffer discrimination because their race has been despised, and also a political right to speak their own mind on matters of public controversy. It would be wrong for government to discriminate against them or to censor their political speech even if that would for some reason benefit the rest of the community. In my view, the list of constitutional rights in the United States Constitution, as these have been interpreted by American courts over recent decades, does a reasonably good job of identifying and protecting the political rights that flow from the two principles of dignity and converting those political rights into legal rights. So do the constitutional documents and international covenants of many other nations and of international communities, in part because they were able to learn from American constitutional practice, just as America can now learn from theirs.

Nevertheless, we must now notice that nations differ strikingly about which political rights to recognize in that way. Even those nations that belong to the same general political culture as our own disagree with us in important matters. In Britain and several other European nations, for example, people have a legal right not to be publicly insulted because of their race; that right is protected by laws making "hate speech" a crime. In the United States, on the contrary, people have a constitutional right publicly to insult anyone they like, by denigrating that person's race or any other group to which he belongs, so long as they do not provoke a riot or incite others to criminal acts. This reflects a good-faith difference in understanding the two principles of dignity: in America, but not in Europe, the reigning opinion holds that respecting people's personal responsibility for their own values means allowing them to challenge even the most fundamental assumptions of democratic society, including the assumption that people's lives are of equal intrinsic value and importance.

The differences in the political rights recognized by nations of radically different moral and religious culture are of course even greater. In many political communities women are subject to a variety of disabilities and constraints that to Americans seem to signal that women are not regarded as of equal importance in those communities. In many communities rights of political participation that we take to be axiomatic are unknown; many states are not even formally democratic, and many of those that claim to be democratic permit only one political party and deny rights of freedom of press and speech that we think indispensable to a genuine democracy. On the other hand, as I said, the United States is widely criticized for not recognizing rights that are firmly recorded in some of the constitutions of many other, particularly newer, countries—social and economic rights, as these are called, to decent housing, medical care, and even jobs.

Human Rights. Now we may ask how human rights differ from the important political rights we have just been considering. I do not mean to ask—yet—which particular rights we should count as human rights. I mean rather to ask how we should understand the idea of a human right so as to justify the common assumption that human rights are political rights but special and very important kinds of political rights. Violations of even important political rights do not ordinarily justify other nations' invading the offending nation or deliberately damaging its economy. Writers are now in jail in Germany, for example, for charging that the Jews largely invented the Holocaust. Americans might criticize Germany for infringing in that way what we take to be a very important political right of free speech, but no one would think that this gives the United States grounds for invading Germany or for imposing trade sanctions against it. When other governments violate what we take to be not only political but human rights, however—when they jail and torture their critics or systematically hunt out and kill members of a minority religion or race—we at least contemplate the possibility of grave sanctions to try to stop these crimes.

So the distinction between political and human rights is very important in practice, and political philosophers disagree about how it should be drawn. Some of them recommend an empirical rather than a judgmental test; they suggest that we designate as human rights only those political rights that are very widely recognized in the practices of nations of all major religious and political cultures. The appeal of that approach is obvious: it protects us against the charge that our conception of human rights is parochial or drawn from a single cultural tradition. But its disadvantage is equally obvious. It would bar us from claiming that patent injustices like wholesale and crippling discrimination against minorities or women, which are traditional in some cultures, are violations of human rights. It would rob the concept of a human right of much of its critical force.

If we are to justify the special role that the idea of human rights plays in domestic and international politics, we must define human rights more critically. Other philosophers therefore suggest that human rights are different from ordinary political rights because the former are in some way more important to people. That suggestion faces a different kind of difficulty, however. We treat all the rights that figure in political argument as of very great importance—we insist that they act as trumps over normal political justification—and we explain that they have that great importance because violations would offend one of the principles that we take to define human dignity. What could be more important than that? If we think that Germany's laws that infringe free speech violate the dignity of its citizens, then why do we not count them as violations of human rights? Why are we then not justified in invading Germany to stop this practice?

We do better to explain the idea of human rights, I suggest, not by trying to establish grades of damage that governments inflict when they make good-faith mistakes in identifying people's moral rights but instead by distinguishing good-faith mistakes made by governments that respect human dignity in principle from those acts that show only contempt for or indifference to human dignity. The fundamental human right, we should say, is the right to be treated with a certain *attitude*: an attitude that expresses the understanding that each person is a human being whose dignity matters. A government can respect that human right even if it makes mistakes in identifying which more concrete political rights it must respect, so long as its mistake is honest. The two principles we have identified give minimum content to that popular idea. Someone's most basic human right, from which all the other human rights flow, is his right to be treated by those in power in a way that is not inconsistent with their accepting that his life is of intrinsic importance and that he has a personal responsibility for realizing value in his own life. Of course, accepting these principles means understanding the limits of what they might intelligibly be thought to countenance. It would not excuse a nation from genocide if its leaders believed that it was good for the people slaughtered to die so that they could be converted to the true faith in heaven. No one who understood the meaning of people being in charge of their own lives could think that that policy respected that principle.

This account of human rights has so far been necessarily very abstract, and I must now try to illustrate it with concrete examples. The basic requirement that government show respect for human dignity functions in two ways, and the distinction between these is of great practical importance. First, that basic requirement is the source of what we might call *baseline* human rights: the concrete rights, like the right not to be tortured, that set limits to how any government may act. These rights forbid acts that could not be justified by any intelligible interpretation of the ideas that people's lives are of equal intrinsic value and that they have a personal responsibility for their own lives. They are the concrete rights that human rights covenants and treaties try to identify.

But, second, the basic requirement has a further, continuing, and distinct force. It forbids any government to act toward anyone in a way that contradicts its *own* understanding of those values—the understanding embedded in its own laws and practices—because that contradiction would just as dramatically deny respect for the humanity of its victims.

Baseline Violations

People and nations can disagree widely but nevertheless in good faith about the best interpretation of each of the two principles of human dignity. That is why different nations recognize somewhat different political rights to enact as legal or constitutional rights. The American understanding of the requirements of personal responsibility, as announced by its Supreme Court, differs from the European understanding and even more dramatically from the understanding in more distant cultures. Germany acts in good faith in punishing those who deny the Holocaust even though, in the opinion of Americans who accept their own traditions, it acts wrongly. It is mistaken about political rights, American lawyers think, but it would be unreasonable for them to deny that it has at least acted on an intelligible understanding of what it means to respect people's equal importance and their personal responsibility.

But some acts of government are so obviously inconsistent with the principles of human dignity that they cannot be thought to be justified by any intelligible conception of those principles. We must draft our core list of human rights to restrict violations to acts of that character. Of course there is room for disagreement about where the line is to be drawn; there is no mechanical test.

That explains why people disagree as they do about, for example, whether human rights include economic rights. But it also explains the great measure of agreement we have achieved in identifying at least some acts as plainly in violation of human rights.

Start with the first principle of dignity, the principle that declares the intrinsic and equal importance of every human life, and start with obvious cases. The most glaring example of contempt for this principle lies in blatant prejudice and discrimination: in assumptions of supposed superiority of one caste over another, of believers over infidels, of Aryans over Semites, or of whites over blacks. It is most horribly evident in the ambitions of genocide. Sometimes the contempt is more personal; people in power sometimes humiliate, rape, or torture their victims just as a demonstration of contempt or, what comes to the same thing, just for amusement. That is what happened to America's prisoners at Abu Ghraib. No nation that supposes that some people are of inferior stock or that condones humiliation and torture for amusement can even begin to claim that it embraces an intelligible conception of human dignity.

Now look briefly at the second principle, which insists that individuals have a personal responsibility to determine the values that define success in their lives. That principle supports the traditional liberal rights of free speech and expression, conscience, political activity, and religion that most human rights documents include. I said earlier that different nations and cultures take different views about how those liberal rights should be defined and protected. Societies also differ about what we might call surface paternalism. Most of us think that compulsory education until late adolescence and mandatory seat belts are permissible forms of paternalism because the first unqualifiedly enhances rather than diminishes a person's capacity to take charge of his own life and the second only helps people to achieve what they actually want, in spite of moments of acknowledged weakness. Some societies are more paternalistic than that but do not violate human rights unless the level of interference could not plausibly be understood in that way. These different political cultures, we might say, take different views about how the personal responsibility of individuals is to be protected.

But once again some acts of government express not a good-faith effort to define and enforce that responsibility but rather a denial of personal responsibility altogether. Governments that forbid the exercise of any but a designated religion or that punish heresy or blasphemy or deny in principle the right of free speech or of the press violate human rights for that reason. So do governments that intimidate, kill, or torture people because they hate or want to change their political opinions. Orwell's novel *1984* remains the classic account of government that usurps an individual's own judgment of the values that should define his life and imposes a single collective ethical judgment on everyone. More than two decades after the date of Orwell's projected nightmare, some nations claim the same authority. They too deny the human rights of their members and subjects.

The right not to be tortured has long been thought the paradigm human right, first on everyone's list. Pain is horrible, but torture is not just a matter of pain. It is sometimes inflicted as a grotesque emblem of power and subjugation, and it violates human rights for that reason. But torture is also used as a tactic in defense of security, and then the case against it must be more complicated. Bush's attorney general, Alberto Gonzales, argued in his confirmation hearings that coercive interrogation, which may include various levels of torture, is a particularly effective means of discovering the information we need to save Americans' lives. That claim is controversial: many experts on interrogation believe that information obtained through torture is almost always useless. But we must nevertheless ask whether torture would still violate human rights even if Gonzales is right. Yes, it would, because torture's object is precisely not just to damage but to destroy a human being's power to decide for himself what his loyalty and convictions permit him to do. Offering inducements such as a reduced sentence to an accused criminal in exchange for information, however objectionable this might seem on other grounds, leaves a prisoner's ability to weigh costs and consequences intact. Torture is designed to extinguish that power, to reduce its victim to a screaming animal for whom decision is no longer possible—the most profound insult to his humanity, the most profound outrage of his human rights.

Now consider a much more controversial example. Capital punishment is practiced in the majority of American states. I believe that capital punishment is morally wrong. I also believe (though I know that most American constitutional lawyers disagree) that the Supreme Court was correct in its original holding, which it later reversed, that capital punishment is unconstitutional because it is cruel and unusual punishment and is therefore in violation of the Constitution's Eighth Amendment. But is capital punishment not only morally wrong and unconstitutional but also a violation of human rights? Many people think so; capital punishment is outlawed in many constitutions, and the laws of the European Union forbid the extradition of any accused criminal to a nation in which he might be subject to execution.

But the case that capital punishment violates human rights is at best inconclusive on the baseline test because two distinct sets of belief might be thought to reconcile human dignity with death as punishment. The first holds that the practice is a significant deterrent to murder. If so, then an adequate case can be made that the practice kills the guilty only to save the innocent and so does not deny the equal intrinsic importance of human lives. It might be objected that there is no persuasive evidence that the death penalty has any important deterrent effect. I agree. But it does not follow that any person who claims to think that the death penalty does deter murder must be insincere. The second holds that capital punishment is justified even if it does not deter because the community is entitled to retribution for murder and that killing a murderer brings what is often called, in an odious phrase, "closure" to the relatives of a murder victim and to society at large. Some prominent moralists who are distinguished for their sensitivity to dignity have endorsed this thesis. I find the thesis deeply unattractive, but I cannot say that anyone who accepts it reveals his underlying contempt for human dignity or for the intrinsic value of a human life. There are important arguments on the other side, however. No jury, no matter how fair and circumspect, can wholly eliminate the possibility of having convicted an innocent person, and it might well seem contemptuous of human life to run that risk. In American practice, the death penalty is inflicted disproportionately on black defendants, and it is difficult not to suspect the stain of racism in those decisions. But the case that capital punishment violates human rights seems, as I said, at best inconclusive as a baseline matter. We can understand the opinion of those who think it does, but they would no doubt agree that it would be preposterous for other nations to invade Texas or Florida to stop the practice, even if they were powerful enough to succeed.

Now we may turn, finally, to the issue that immediately concerns us. Do America's policies for combating the terrorist threat violate baseline human rights, the rights any nation, no matter what its traditions and practices, must respect? Certainly torture violates baseline rights, whatever the Bush administration's lawyers may say. Most Americans would agree with that judgment, and the administration formally denies that it tortures its prisoners. So we should now concentrate on the detention policies that the administration concedes it follows and that a great many Americans would defend. We imprison hundreds of people indefinitely without charge or trial on the basis of only an executive determination that these people are dangerous enemies, a determination that is not subject to ordinary review by courts. Does this policy violate those prisoners' baseline human rights?

I shall try to construct an argument on behalf of Americans who think it does not. Our detention policy is based on suppositions of fact that these Americans believe would justify that policy if true and that are not so plainly false that no reasonable person could accept them. America faces a continuing threat of a massively lethal terrorist attack, and our government believes that those it detains would increase this danger if they were released, or that they are withholding information that would help America to reduce the threat, or both. That may not be true of some of the detainees. They may be innocent and pose no threat. But it is too risky to allow judges to make that determination after ordinary criminal trials because we know that such trials sometimes allow dangerous people to go free.

It is true, the argument concedes, that America must nevertheless show respect for the human dignity of the detainees. But the military does provide a process for reviewing the status of the Guantánamo detainees: it conducts hearings in which military officers examine the question, independently for each detainee, whether he was indeed an enemy combatant and if so, whether he remains a danger to the United States. A few detainees have in fact been released after such hearings apparently ruled in their favor. True, the hearings do not provide anything like the guarantees and protections that we insist on for our own citizens in normal domestic criminal trials. The detainees are not allowed counsel of their own choice. They are not informed of the evidence against them and hence are given no opportunity to challenge that evidence. There is no review of the tribunals' decisions by judges or anyone outside the executive branch of government: in effect, the military acts as prosecutor, judge, and jury. Nevertheless, according to this argument, these minimal arrangements satisfy baseline human rights because a nation would not provide even that kind of hearing for prisoners it considers security threats unless it recognized them as human beings and accepted a responsibility to protect their dignity.

Many Americans find that a plausible argument. They conclude that the administration's detention practices do not violate the baseline human rights that every nation must observe as a matter of moral imperative. They accept the government's claim that the only pertinent question is whether its detention policies violate our legal commitments under the Geneva Conventions or other treaties, and they also accept the government's assurance that they do not. I disagree, as I said, with the latter judgment; I believe that the Bush government's detention policies do violate its obligations under international law. But what of the deeper moral question? Should we accept the argument I constructed?

Or does our detention practice violate the baseline human rights that any nation, whatever its history, must respect?

We cannot say that any nation that does not offer its ordinary criminal defendants a trial as safe as those the United States allows its ordinary defendants shows contempt for the value of those defendants' lives. Many nations have different criminal procedures from ours. Some of these do not protect the innocent as effectively as our ordinary procedures do, and we cannot say that their practices violate baseline human rights just for that reason. However, the Guantánamo hearings are less safe than even the most relaxed procedures of nations whose systems of criminal justice we respect and also less safe than the criminal procedures that many international human rights conventions demand. In early 2006, five inspectors of the United Nations Human Rights Commission declared that the Guantánamo camp should be closed because of its human rights violations. Prime Minister Tony Blair of Great Britain, America's strongest ally in Iraq, called the camp an "anomaly," and Britain's attorney general, Lord Goldsmith, said that the proper way to deal with terrorist activity "is fair trial" and that the military tribunals the administration has proposed would not provide "a fair trial by standards we would accept." So the argument that America's detention procedures show sufficient respect for human dignity to satisfy baseline human rights seems at best weak and inconclusive. In any case, however, that is not the only human rights challenge those procedures must face.

Bad-Faith Violations

The most basic of human rights, I said, is the right to be treated by government with a certain attitude: with the respect due a human being. We have been considering baseline human rights—those more concrete rights that any nation must respect no matter what its culture or traditions. But the fundamental human right is not exhausted by these baseline rights; it requires more of particular nations because those nations' practices may show that they regard a kind of treatment as contemptuous even though other nations do not. If so, those nations deny respect when they treat anyone in that way. Suppose a community has established and protects a particularly vigorous version of freedom of speech. If that doctrine represents its considered opinion of what human dignity requires, then it could not defend denying an equal freedom to any subgroup within the nation—or, indeed, to foreigners—as a good-faith attempt to respect the latter's human rights. If a nation's practice shows that it takes respect for fundamental principle to require more generous protection against imprisoning the innocent than other nations concede to their citizens, it must honor that conviction for everyone who falls into its power. If it does not, then it does not treat those it makes exceptions as fully human.

So the second test that the idea of human rights imposes, the test of consistency of respect for dignity, is a much more stringent test for the United States than the first one. The second test forbids government to act in ways that cannot be justified under the conception of dignity that the nation has embraced. The ordinary criminal-justice practices of the United States establish what we collectively believe that respect for human dignity requires for those accused of crimes, and so we do show contempt for terrorist suspects when we deny that respect to them. It would no doubt be very useful—and would certainly improve our collective safety, perhaps by a good deal—if our police could, as a matter of course, lock up ordinary citizens they thought dangerous to other people's safety without the expense, delay, and possible embarrassment of a trial. Indeed it would be extremely useful in our war against drugs to be able to incarcerate people we had no reason to think had committed a crime at all, particularly if we thought they had information about the drug trade that we might induce them to share with us. We refuse our police those options, useful though they might be, because we think people have a right not to be injured in that very serious way even when that would make us safer and help to rid our community of very serious dangers, including the curse of drugs.

We deny ourselves this improved security because we think that depriving someone of his liberty by locking him away is a crude violation both of his status as someone whose life has intrinsic value and of his responsibility to lead his own life. Imprisonment is an extreme form of slavery. We could not justify imposing this terrible slavery on someone just marginally to improve the safety of others unless we counted his life as unimportant next to theirs. So a policy of jailing suspected criminals without charge or trial, or jailing people who have not committed a crime but whom our police judge to be dangerous, would violate what we take the dignity of human beings to require.

Of course we sometimes do inflict that slavery—even death—on those we accuse of crime, and we do it entirely to make the rest of us safer. We do that whenever we convict someone of a crime after a fair trial and punish him in those ways. But we nevertheless act consistently with our conception of human dignity because if our trials really are fair, then we can reasonably think that we have not judged the criminal's life as less important than anyone else's. We have not selected him to damage for the good of the rest of us; he has selected himself for that role by his deliberate decision to damage others for his own good or purposes. This justification of our treatment of the convicted criminal turns entirely on the fairness and adequacy of our procedures for judging whether the criminal has in fact selected himself in that way. That is why we make such efforts to ensure that our procedures are as fair as we can reasonably make them; that is the true explanation of our ancient assumption that it is much better to acquit the guilty, however dangerous, than to convict the innocent. We might, it is true, have developed different and less demanding standards of fairness in our criminal procedures. We might have come to think that allowing the police themselves to try those they have arrested without allowing the prisoners to know or confront the evidence against them and with no judicial review of conviction was a sufficiently fair procedure in murder cases. We might now be safer if we had formed and had followed that opinion. But we did not come to think that. On the contrary, we have come to think, as a nation, that any such procedure would not be sufficiently fair to justify the grave damage and insult of imprisonment.

We also detain people without trial in a very different kind of circumstance: when we are fighting a war and we capture enemy soldiers who have committed no crime by fighting against us. In these circumstances, our practice is governed by international law, which permits us to hold such soldiers until the end of hostilities, but only under the relatively benign conditions stipulated by the Geneva Conventions, which include living arrangements equal to those who are guarding them and forbid even limited forms of coercive interrogation. We claim that those we have imprisoned at Guantánamo and elsewhere as suspected terrorists are not entitled to those arrangements and that we may hold them until the United States is no longer at risk from terrorism (which may well be for the rest of their lives) because they have acted illegally. We treat them as criminals, though we refuse them the rights of criminals, including the most basic right to be accused of and tried for their alleged crimes. Once again, this cannot be justified if we assume that our ordinary criminal law states what we take to be the essential rights of an accused, because we cannot then claim to be acting in good faith in our protestation that this is all that the essential rights of those we suspect of terrorism demand. Instead we show only that we do not regard them as fully human.

Security and Honor

I have now set out an argument that America's policy of imprisoning suspected terrorists indefinitely violates human rights. The argument begins in a conception of human rights that is grounded in the two basic principles of human dignity. It demands, first, that any government, whatever its traditions and practices, act consistently with some good-faith understanding of the equal intrinsic importance of people's lives and of their personal responsibility for their own lives. It also demands, second, that nations that have developed their own distinct understanding of what these standards require not deny the benefit of that understanding to anyone. The latter demand is particularly strong in the case of the United States, and it means that, for us, our policy of indefinite imprisonment without trial violates the human rights of those we imprison.

That argument contradicts what a great many Americans think, and so we must now consider how they might oppose it. What argument could they construct to a contrary conclusion? They might, first and most fundamentally, reject the theory of human rights in which my argument begins. Some nations and some movements indeed would reject that theory because it is grounded in principles of human dignity that are far from universally shared. But think what it means to reject the principles. The Bosnian Serbs said that their genocidal programs did not violate human rights because the Muslims were not really human, and the Hutu said much the same about the Tutsis they slaughtered. If we are to accept the idea of human rights at all, then we must take a stand somewhere about who is a human being and what it means to treat someone with human dignity. We cannot be ecumenical all the way down; we must give content to these phrases, and we must rely on our own convictions to do that.

Some might object that if we insist on the conception of dignity I defined, we must be assuming that there is objective truth to be had in the realms of ethics and morality. I agree. But we must make that assumption because the opposite, skeptical claim is philosophically indefensible. I have tried to explain why in other writing,[5] and I assume that rejecting that skepticism is part of the common ground we share. Conservatives sometimes say that liberals are moral skeptics; just after his elevation, Pope Benedict XVI said that liberals embrace moral relativism. This is a mistake: both our two supposed political cultures, save for a few misguided philosophers on each side, reject relativism with equal conviction.

So I shall assume that the millions of Americans who would reject my argument would not reject the theory of human rights on which it is based. What other arguments might they make? They might challenge my claim that because Americans insist on certain procedures in their domestic criminal law, it follows that they believe that these procedures are indispensable to protecting human dignity. Certainly it would be implausible to treat certain aspects of our criminal procedures as carrying that implication. For some time the Supreme Court insisted that evidence could not used against an accused criminal at his trial—no matter how persuasive that evidence was of his guilt—if the police had obtained the evidence illegally. That rule, which has since been withdrawn, was justified as a useful deterrent to police irregularity; no one supposed that introducing genuine evidence of an accused criminal's guilt denies the equal importance of his life even when the police have obtained that evidence in an illegitimate way.

But the rules forbidding imprisonment without trial and requiring that an accused be permitted to know the charges and evidence against him plainly belong in a different category. They serve no secondary, instrumental purpose; they are designed to prevent what we believe would be a grave injustice. We pay a considerable price in security by forswearing preventive detention for those we have reason to think are likely to commit violent crimes in the future and by allowing those we believe have committed such crimes an opportunity to defend themselves with the aid of skilled counsel and be judged by officials who have not prejudged their guilt. It makes no sense to suppose that we pay that price for any reason except to prevent a grave injustice.

Those who defend the administration might argue, somewhat differently, that nationality makes a difference, that our ordinary rules of criminal process reflect our convictions only about what we owe our own fellow citizens and that we might in perfect good faith suppose that respecting the dignity of foreigners requires less by way of constraints on our police and military power. Justice Robert Jackson, a very distinguished Supreme Court justice who was a prosecutor at the Nuremberg trials of Nazis after World War II, once said that it would be silly to think that enemy nationals were entitled to the same rights under the American Constitution as are American citizens. But the idea of human rights would lose its meaning if a nation owed nothing to foreigners. We need a theory of citizenship that sets out and justifies a distinction between what a nation may do or refrain from doing for or to its own members and what it must do for or not do to anyone. I cannot construct such a theory now, but I can describe its rudiments.

Citizens must of course have unique privileges of participation in government: voting and holding office. Otherwise there would be no point to the distinction between citizens and aliens. Citizens may also have special rights to the benefits of residence: rights to enter the country when abroad, for example, which aliens, who may be refused a visa, do not have. Government has special responsibilities of care and concern for citizens and other residents, responsibilities that I will explore in chapter 4. A nation's economic policy may be designed primarily to favor its own residents, and it may distribute welfare and other benefits to them that it does not distribute to people living in other countries. In all this, a nation may—and to some degree must—discriminate in favor of its own citizens and therefore against those not its own. But the deliberate infliction of injury is different, and government has no right or authority deliberately to injure foreigners for reasons or in circumstances in which it would not be permitted to injure its own citizens. This is emphatically true when the injury is grave. The domain of human rights has no place for passports.

Finally those who wish to defend the Bush administration may concede that its detention policies do violate the human rights of our prisoners but may nevertheless insist that we must "balance" the human rights of others against our own right to security from terror, so that we may properly ignore the rights of foreigners when the danger foreigners pose is sufficiently great. To be sure, it is often said that no rights can be absolute, that there are always circumstances in which government is justified in compromising or ignoring them. The great charters of human rights, including the European Convention on Human Rights, recognize this fact by burdening many of the rights that they list with important qualifications; the European Convention, for example, identifies free speech as a basic human right but then adds that governments are entitled to abridge that right when this is necessary to protect public order or morals. These qualifications were the result of political compromises that served to reassure countries hesitating to embrace the convention. But they do seem to suggest that human rights are not absolute and in that way to challenge my claims that human rights are powerful trumps over otherwise legitimate government aims.

There is an important ambiguity in the claim that human rights are not absolute, however. Sometimes it means that the description of a right in some document or in a common phrase is only an abstraction and must be refined before we know exactly what it means in concrete circumstances. We say that freedom of speech is a human right, but no one thinks that anyone's human rights are violated by reasonable restrictions placed on the time and place of demonstrations and parades. We say that free speech is a right, but we owe ourselves a more precise accounting of what that right is; we might decide, for example, that it is the right not to be censored in the expression of political ideas on the ground that such ideas are in themselves wrong or dangerous, which explains why restrictions on the timing of parades are acceptable. That is, once we have a careful account of exactly what the human right in question really is, we no longer find it embarrassing to claim that right as absolute, to say that it brooks no violation.

Sometimes, however, the claim that even human rights are not absolute means something more dramatic and more pertinent: that in a sufficiently grave emergency, a government is justified in violating even the most basic and fundamental human rights even after these have been precisely stated. There is a stock example whose familiarity may have deadened its force. Suppose we have captured a terrorist who we know has planted a nuclear bomb timed to explode in two hours somewhere in Manhattan. It would be absurd, people say, not to torture him if we thought torture would force him to tell us where the bomb is in time to defuse it. Let us now accept, if only for the sake of this discussion, that it is morally permissible to violate human rights in a sufficiently grave emergency like this one. Then our question becomes: how grave must the emergency be?

Remember our premises. In chapter 1 I said that we damage ourselves, not just our victim, when we ignore his humanity, because in denigrating his intrinsic value we denigrate our own. We compromise our dignity and our self-respect. So we must put the hurdle of emergency very high indeed. We must take care not to define "emergency" as simply "great danger" or to suppose that any act that improves our own security, no matter how marginally, is for that reason justified. We must hold to a very different virtue: the old-fashioned virtue of courage. Sacrificing self-respect in the face of danger is a particularly shameful form of cowardice. We show courage in our domestic criminal law and practice: we increase the statistical risk that each of us will suffer from violent crime when we forbid preventive detention and insist on fair trials for everyone accused of crime. We must show parallel courage when the danger comes from abroad because our dignity is at stake in the same way.

Now notice the crucial dimensions of the stock example about the ticking nuclear bomb hidden in Manhattan. The danger is both horrific and certain; we know that our victim is responsible for that danger, and we assume that if we torture him and he yields, we can remove the danger. None of that is true about our policy of imprisonment without charge or trial in Guantánamo and our other bases around the world. We are in danger of another devastating attack, to be sure. But there is no reason yet to think that the danger approaches certainty or that our violations of human rights are well calculated to end or even significantly to reduce that danger. We gathered our prisoners indiscriminately. We erred on the side of inclusion; anyone we thought might be dangerous or might have useful information was swept up. We have already released, under diplomatic and judicial pressure, several of those we held in Guantánamo for many months. In each case, we stated that we are now satisfied that it is not necessary to hold the prisoners. Of course the public does not know what information the interrogation has so far secured. But the criticism of our detention policies has been so intense, at home as well as in other countries, that I suspect the government would have made more precise claims about the value of that information if it could have done so.

We are in great danger of falling into the trap I just warned against: thinking that anything that improves America's security, however marginally or speculatively, is wise policy. That makes a terrified prudence the only virtue we recognize; it sacrifices courage and dignity to a mean and cowardly prejudice that our own security is the only thing that matters. We do not make that mistake in our own lives or our own domestic law, and it is not plain that the danger from terrorism is greater, all in all, than the dangers from drugs, serial killers, and other crimes. But the threat to our dignity is certainly greater now, and we must stand together to defeat that greater danger. The metaphor of balancing rights against security is, as I have said, very misleading. A different metaphor would be much more appropriate: we must balance our security against our honor. Are we now so frightened that honor means nothing?

CHAPTER 3

RELIGION AND DIGNITY

Politics and Religion

A MERICA'S RELIGIOSITY is not new; America has
been a religious country since its beginning. A great
many more Americans than Europeans believe in an afterlife, the
Virgin birth, and the biblical account of the creation, both of the
universe and of human beings. Islamic nations are also very religious, of course, and our declared war on terror often seems an
anachronistic religious war. Indeed, Bush once called it a crusade.
Historians debate why religion has been so important here; many
now think that religion has prospered, paradoxically, because
America has no official or established religion as several other
democracies have. An established church sucks in fringe sects and
tends toward ecumenism rather than fundamentalism; in the ab-
sence of an official church, fundamentalist sects thrive, and such
sects are the ones most likely to have political agendas.

What is different now—and has frightened many people not
just in America but around the world—is the political militancy,
aggressiveness, and apparent success of fundamentalist religion.
Religion played a deplorable role in American politics in the past,
but after John Kennedy's election in 1960—no Catholic had been

elected president before him—the partisan use of religion seemed taboo. The inhibition began to evaporate in the Reagan years, however, and now it seems to be gone. Roman Catholic and evangelical priests openly called for John Kerry's defeat, and a group of bishops said that any Catholic voting for him should be excommunicated. Bush's campaign was full of references to God, and his second inaugural address amazed the world with its explicit religiosity.

The evangelical community claimed credit for Bush's victory and called on him to repay its efforts. The Reverend Bob Jones III, president of Bob Jones University, is an extreme figure, but his triumphal tone was not untypical. He wrote Bush, "In your re-election, God has graciously granted America—though she doesn't deserve it—a reprieve from the agenda of paganism. You have been given a mandate. . . . Put your agenda on the front burner and let it boil. You owe the liberals nothing. They despise you because they despise your Christ."[1]

It is unclear that the reverend was right in his claim that the election gave Bush a mandate for born-again Christian government; it is doubtful how many people voted for Bush primarily on religious grounds. A much-quoted exit poll suggested that the most important issue for many Bush voters was what the poll labeled "moral values," and many commentators assumed this meant religious values. But "moral values" is an exceptionally opaque description, and other commentators think Bush won narrowly mainly because people thought he was tougher on terrorists. We do not know yet, and may never know. Religion did play at least an important role in the election, however, and aspiring politicians—Democratic as well as Republican—are plainly tempted to make much more explicit use of religious appeal and rhetoric than would be tolerated in other nations of similar democratic and economic maturity.[2]

Parents and school boards across the country are pressing teachers to make their students aware of alternatives to the Darwinian theory of evolution, such as the so-called intelligent design theory, which a federal judge appointed by President Bush declared only a disguised form of Christian religious instruction. When Florida judges ruled that life support could be terminated for Terri Schiavo, a young woman who had been in a persistent vegetative state for many months, politicians declared that the judges were defying God's will. Congress tried to intervene, and Tom DeLay, then the Republican House majority leader, who has since been indicted for various crimes, produced the stunningly insensitive claim that God had given her misery to the country "to help elevate the visibility of what is going on in America."[3] Not everyone who is religious has joined this rush to political religiosity. John Danforth is a Christian minister who was a Republican senator from Missouri for eighteen years and for a time Bush's ambassador to the United Nations. The Republican party, he said recently, "has gone so far in adopting a sectarian agenda that it has become the political extension of a religious movement." "As a senator," he continued, "I worried every day about the size of the federal deficit. I did not spend a single minute worrying about the effect of gays on the institution of marriage. Today it seems to be the other way around."[4] But very few active politicians have spoken out against the phenomenon Danforth deplored.

Abortion made the difference in turning evangelicalism, which has long been socially powerful in large parts of America, into a more potent political force. The Supreme Court's decision in *Roe v. Wade* in 1973 gave the religious Right an issue its members took to be of mortal importance, an issue that could organize a hitherto disparate minority into a powerful political movement. Abortion swept other issues in its wake: stem-cell research is on its own a much less potent issue, but the abortion argument had so hardened ideological positions that the so-called pro-life movement had to condemn any use of fetal tissue even in ways that promised to save lives on a grand scale. In 2004 these fiercely galvanizing issues were joined by gay marriage. The spectacle of marriage between people of the same sex, which the Massachusetts Supreme Court said the state was unable to prevent, is viscerally revolting to millions of people; it is particularly shocking to those who believe they have religious sanction for their revulsion.

These two issues, abortion and gay marriage, have been the most dramatic magnets drawing evangelicalism into politics. But they have spawned a much broader spectrum of causes, and religious conservatives now seem to aim at nothing short of a general absorption of Christianity into America's public life. Once again, however, there has been no effort to construct a genuine argument about these developments. The pronouncements of the religious Right make no attempt to appeal to those who do not share the faith; they are unabashedly theological. The liberal side of the argument has been equally apocalyptic. Garry Wills published an article in the *New York Times* two days after the 2004 presidential election titled "The Day the Enlightenment Went Out," calling Bush's fundamentalist campaign a "jihad."[5]

Two Models

The clash of opinion that divides us on this issue is not about the truth of religion or about any tenet of faith. Many of those who are appalled by the program and tactics of the religious Right are themselves, like Danforth, devout. The clash is over the role that religion should play in politics, religion, and public life. How can we construct a genuine argument rather than just a brute confrontation about that?

We might try to do this issue by issue. Should abortion and stem-cell research be banned? Should gay marriage be recognized? Is it acceptable for our political leaders to appeal to a god and to that god's will to justify their policies when Americans disagree about whether there is a god, and if so, what his, her, or its will is? Should prayer be either required or permitted in public schools? Should our pledge of allegiance refer to "one nation under God"? Should government issue education vouchers that parents can use to send their children to private instead of public schools when we know that these will be used primarily to support parochial schools? Should cities and towns be allowed to exhibit religious symbols like Christmas trees and menorahs on public property?

Should a judge be allowed to place a tablet containing the Ten Commandments in his courtroom? Should Darwin and the big bang theory of cosmology be taught in our public schools? If so, should teachers be instructed to say that some reputable scientists reject these theories and believe that there is good scientific evidence that an intelligent author designed the universe and human beings? Should there be exemptions from general obligations or regulations for those whose religion requires or forbids a legally forbidden or required act? Can an atheist who hates war be a conscientious objector? Should Indian tribes who use peyote in their rites be exempt from laws banning peyote because it is a hallucinogenic drug? Should doctors be legally allowed to remove the life support of someone in a persistent vegetative state? Should they be legally allowed to help someone who is terminally ill and in great discomfort to kill himself? This is only a partial list of the issues we now debate about religion and government, and it will soon be out of date. We do not know what tomorrow's cutting-edge issue about church and state will be.

We might discuss each of these issues in turn and try to anticipate other issues. In fact, I shall discuss some of them. But it will be more illuminating first to distinguish two polar attitudes that define the general problem, two models that we might adopt as ideal types to follow in confronting more concrete issues one by one. Americans agree on one crucially important principle: our government must be tolerant of all peaceful religious faiths and also of people of no faith. But from what base should our tolerance spring? Should we be a religious nation, collectively committed to the values of faith and worship, but with tolerance for religious minorities including nonbelievers? Or should we be a nation committed to thoroughly secular government but with tolerance and accommodation for people of religious faith? A religious nation that tolerates nonbelief? Or a secular nation that tolerates religion? In practice, a nation might well compromise between these two models, drawing some institutions and rules from each. Indeed American practice reflects such a mixture of the two models now. But the two models reflect contrary principles of political morality, and though we may be forced by practical politics to construct some compromise between them, any serious argument about the place of religion in government and public life must in the end be a debate about these competing ideals.

Israel has chosen to be a tolerant religious nation. It has an official religion—Judaism—though in principle it offers religious freedom to all faiths. France, with its complex background of priests and Jacobins, has firmly chosen the second model: it is a tolerant secular nation. Jacques Chirac, its president, attended Pope John Paul II's funeral and flew French flags at half-mast, but he was sharply criticized in France for doing so. Britain is a more complex case, but it leans strongly to the second model as well, at least in practice. Its established church owes more to its love of tradition and ceremony, I think, than to any genuine shared national religious commitment, and it would be astounding—and politically fatal—for a prime minister to claim religious authority for state policy. Liberal Americans thought that their country had also chosen to be a tolerant secular state a few decades ago when our civics teachers proudly quoted Jefferson's maxim about the wall between church and state and the Supreme Court took prayer out of the schools. But recent political success has emboldened the religious Right to try to turn America into a tolerant religious state instead.

We must be clear about what is at stake in that choice, and it will be helpful, at least initially, to use a distinction beloved of American constitutional scholars. Our First Amendment forbids our government to establish religion, and it then requires that that government guarantee the free exercise "thereof." Scholars treat these as independent and, indeed, sometimes antagonistic requirements. Establishment refers to state endorsement or sponsorship of religion, and free exercise to individual freedom of religious practice. We can contrast the two models on each of these two dimensions.

The Establishment of Religion

A tolerant religious vision interprets the requirement that government must not establish religion to mean that it must not establish any one of the discrete faiths to which many of its citizens belong as the official state religion. It must not embrace Catholicism, Judaism, or the Baptist sect as the nation's faith. But a tolerant religious state does openly acknowledge and support, as official state policy, religion as such; it declares religion to be an important positive force in making people and society better. It celebrates a generalized monotheism. A tolerant religious society therefore has no embarrassment about reference to a single god in its official pledge of allegiance; on the contrary, it would regard omitting such a reference as unpatriotic. Nor is it embarrassed by direct appeals to that god's will as justifying policy, as when Bush said in his second inaugural address that in protecting liberty abroad he was serving the "author" of liberty. (He didn't, I think, mean John Stuart Mill.) A tolerant religious society will accept only one reason for curtailing its rhetorical and financial support for religion—protecting the freedom of dissenters and nonbelievers. It will not prohibit or penalize the practice of any faith or the practice of none. But it will not shrink from declaring, as an official public conviction of the nation, that nonbelievers are deeply mistaken.

In a tolerant secular society the state must also be permissive about religion; it must not make the peaceful practice of even fundamentalist religion illegal. It is no more officially committed to atheism than it is to religion; it is collectively neutral on the subject of whether there is a god or gods or which religion is best, if any is. It would not tolerate any religious—or antireligious— reference or insinuation in its official ceremonies and statements of policy. On the contrary, it would take care to insulate its patriotic oaths, allegiances, and celebrations from any religious or antireligious dimension. It would not outlaw Christmas trees or menorahs, of course, but it would not install or permit them on public property. It would not penalize people of faith any more than it would atheists; it would not discriminate against either group in the provision of public services. But it would be wary of state programs that particularly benefited religious organizations, like providing general education vouchers that parents could then use to pay the fees of parochial schools. It would follow something like the rule that constitutional lawyers call the *Lemon* test because the Supreme Court announced it in a case of that name. This test forbids any state program that is either intended to or that does operate to the particular advantage of a religious organization. Justice Sandra Day O'Connor elaborated the second part of that test in this way "[T]he effect prong of the *Lemon* test is properly interpreted not to require invalidation of a government practice merely because it in fact causes, even as a primary effect, advancement or inhibition of religion. . . . What is crucial is that the government practice not have the effect of communicating a message of government endorsement or disapproval of religion."[6]

We may sharpen the contrast between the two models by focusing on the seminally divisive issue of public-school prayer. In a tolerant religious community, there can be no objection in principle to teachers' leading schoolchildren in prayer. Such prayers must of course be designed to be as ecumenical as possible; the Lord's Prayer, which I recited every day in school, would serve. However, a tolerant religious state must take care not to coerce children into reciting even so ecumenical a prayer as that, because it must leave them free to reject religion altogether. Perhaps simply allowing children who so choose to remain seated and silent would protect them from coercion. But perhaps not; it might be that children would be reluctant to identify themselves as outsiders in that way and would be pressured into reciting prayers in which they did not believe. Whether prayers would in the end be permitted in public schools in a tolerant religious society would depend on how that empirical psychological issue is resolved.[7]

In a tolerant secular society, however, that empirical question would be irrelevant. It would be seen as wrong in principle to make any state institution such as a public school the venue of any exercise of any religion. Of course, a tolerant secular state would permit teaching about religion in public schools; no liberal education would be satisfactory without instruction in the doctrines of and differences between the main religious traditions, the history of religious divisions, and contemporary controversies about what role religion should play in public life. But a tolerant secular society would not allow its institutions to be used for practicing, as distinct from studying, religion.

The Free Exercise of Religion

Since each of our two model communities is tolerant of all peaceful religious practice, including no religious practice, we might think that they agree about the scope of religious freedom. But in fact they disagree deeply about what that freedom includes or at least presupposes. Neither model would impose any ban on the peaceful practice of any religion. But recognizing a right to religious freedom requires settling on at least a rough account of the origin and basis of that right, and the two communities must disagree about that. People who support a tolerant religious society might be tempted to declare the right of religious freedom to be sui generis, a special right reflecting the special importance of religion. They might therefore be tempted to a very narrow view of that right: that it encompasses only the freedom to worship a supernatural being under one description rather than another, or in one church dedicated to such worship rather than another, and also the freedom to reject altogether the existence or importance of any such creature. The right of religious freedom so understood would not presuppose any more general right from which it is drawn. It would not presuppose a general right to decide matters of fundamental ethical importance for oneself: the right to submit to an abortion, for example, or to practice homosexuality free from any particular penalty, to engage in stem-cell research, or to end one's own life when terminally ill and in pain. Indeed, a tolerant religious society might prohibit or penalize all such practices on explicitly religious grounds: it might condemn homosexuality as against God's will as recognized in all major monotheistic religious traditions, for example. These prohibitions would not violate the free exercise of religion even if they were justified in that religious way because the practices in question are not, for a tolerant religious society, in any sense *religious* practices.

A tolerant secular society cannot accept such a narrow account of the ground of freedom of religion, however. Although a tolerant religious society can find a special justification for that right in the special value of religion, a tolerant secular society cannot because it does not, as a community, attach any special value to religion as a phenomenon. It knows that many of its members do attach great importance to their freedom to choose their own religious commitments and life, and it is of course anxious to respect that conviction. But it also knows that other members attach comparable importance to making other choices about how to live—about sexuality or procreation, for instance—that reflect their own different convictions about what lives would be good for them. So any right to freedom of choice that gave special protection to religious people or religious practices would be regarded in such a society as discrimination in their favor because it would leave other people open to constraints on their freedom in the exercise of choices that, for them, reflect values of the same ethical character and function as the religious values of religious people. A tolerant secular community must therefore find its justification for religious freedom in a more basic principle of liberty that generates a more generous conception of the spheres of value in which people must be left free to choose for themselves. It must treat freedom of religion, that is, as one case of a more general right not simply of religious but of ethical freedom.

In chapter 1, in trying to explicate the second principle of human dignity, I offered this rough account of the distinction between ethical and other values: ethical values are those that define why human life has distinct and intrinsic value and how that value is best realized in a particular life. Orthodox religious convictions are plainly ethical on that account, and a tolerant secular society that adopted a right of ethical freedom would of course guarantee freedom of orthodox religious exercise. But it would not limit the scope of the ethical to orthodox religion; it could have no reason for embracing freedom of orthodox worship without also embracing freedom of choice in all ethical matters and therefore freedom of choice with respect to the ethical values that are plainly implicated in decisions about sexual conduct, marriage, and procreation.

Where Do We Stand Now?

Which model does the American Constitution provide? Religious conservatives answer that question by reciting the following history. America was founded as a tolerant religious society and continued to be one until after the Second World War, when unelected judges decided, against the plain wishes of most Americans, to transform it into a tolerant secular state. So the religious political movement now under way, which aims to wipe away what the unelected judges did, is not revolutionary but rather designed to restore religion to its historic place in American society and government. That is not an unreasonable history. In 1931 the Supreme Court could declare, "We are a Christian people,"[8] and as late as 1952 Justice William O. Douglas, generally counted among the most liberal justices in the Court's history, announced, "We are a religious people whose institutions presuppose a Supreme Being."[9] The decisions that religious conservatives count as hostile to religion came later: in 1962, for instance, when the Court outlawed public-school prayer on the ground—distinctive to the tolerant secular model—that the state has no legitimate business promoting religion.[10]

The tolerant religious view has certainly had strong support on the Supreme Court, particularly recently. Justice Anthony Kennedy spoke for that view in dissenting from a Supreme Court decision that endorsed and applied the *Lemon* test. He said,

"Rather than requiring government to avoid any action that acknowledges or aids religion, the [Constitution] permits government some latitude in recognizing and accommodating the central role religion plays in our society."[11] He specifically rejected the idea that government must do nothing that would make nonreligious people feel like outsiders. He noted that our pledge of allegiance includes a reference to God, and he said that it "borders on sophistry" to suggest that an atheist would not feel "less a member of the political community every time his fellow Americans" recited that phrase. The Constitution, he said, does not require anything more than that government not actually coerce citizens into any religious declaration or observance and that it not actually establish a state religion. That is an extreme statement of the tolerant religious model, but it might accurately state the position of a majority of the justices now serving.

In many other ways that will strike you as more trivial, we seem closer to a tolerant religious model than a tolerant secular one. Our currency declares our collective trust in God, our great institutions of government begin their proceedings with a prayer, and few commentators would expect the Supreme Court to declare the pledge of allegiance's reference to God unconstitutional if it is ever required to decide that issue. It is widely argued that these practices are only ceremonial, only ritual mumblings, like the telephone operator wishing you a nice day. But the Supreme Court would, I think, arouse national fury if it failed finally to sustain the pledge in its present form, and this testifies not to the banality and unimportance of official invocations of God but to their symbolic importance. They reassure religious citizens that they do not live in a fundamentally secular society, a society in which even casual official references to God would be forbidden.

Religion and Narrow Political Liberalism

So liberals cannot claim with any confidence that the secular model is America's historical model. But we must try to frame a debate of principle, not of history. For some time many liberal academic philosophers in America have tried to insulate their discussion of political policy from more general issues of ethical and moral philosophy and in particular from issues of theology. That strategy is based on an attractive hope: that reasonable people in political community will wish to live together on terms of mutual respect and accommodation and will therefore accept the constraints of what the very influential philosopher John Rawls called public reason.[12] They will accept that they must justify collective political decisions to one another in terms that each can understand and whose force each can appreciate given his own comprehensive religious, moral, and ethical beliefs. That constraint would rule out appeals to even an ecumenical religious faith in a community some of whose members reject all religion. It would command a tolerant secular state. So we might try to frame our debate around the question whether we should all accept that constraint of public reason.

Rawls himself described the weakness of his proposal, however. "How is it possible . . . for those of faith . . . to endorse a constitutional regime even when their comprehensive doctrines may not prosper under it, and indeed may decline?"[13] We must look at the matter from the standpoint of such people. Many religious conservatives think that a god is responsible for America's exceptional success and good fortune and that it is both base and dangerous to deny that god public tribute for that grace. Newt Gingrich declared, "We must reestablish that our rights come from our Creator, and that an America that has driven God out of the public arena is an America on the way to decay and defeat."[14] Americans of that opinion cannot separate these religious convictions from their political principles. Their religious convictions *are* political principles. They do not accept private observance as a substitute for public religious endorsement; they want to celebrate their god not just as private worshipers but as citizens. They want to pour their faith into their patriotism so that the two commitments are one. They see no appeal in a principle that tells them to set that transcendent ambition aside in deference to people who do not share their religious faith. They think that such people are in profound error and that the error is willful. They believe not that religion is inaccessible to atheists or that the god they recognize has denied such people his grace, but rather that atheists have stubbornly refused to open their hearts to the truth. Why should they abandon the profound ambitions of their faith simply to satisfy those who persist in that stubbornness?

Moreover, it is hardly plain that it would be desirable for people of religion to keep their convictions divorced from their politics even if that were possible for them. Martin Luther King Jr. was a man of faith, and he invoked his religion to condemn prejudice with great effect; Catholic priests speaking as priests have been vanguard fighters for social justice in Latin America and elsewhere. In any case, however, liberals will not succeed if they ask people of faith to set aside their religious convictions when they take up the role of citizens. That role demands sincerity and authenticity, which is impossible for such people unless they keep their religion very much in mind. The schism over religion in America shows the limitations of Rawls's project of political liberalism, his strategy of insulating political convictions from deeper moral, ethical, and religious conviction.

Our strategy must be different. We must not try to exclude people's most profound convictions from political debate. On the contrary, we must try to achieve a genuine debate within civil society about those profound convictions. Liberals must try to show religious conservatives that their ambition to fuse religion and politics in the way they now propose is an error because it contradicts very basic principles that are also part of their faith. Conservatives must try to show liberals that they are wrong in that judgment. I said in chapter 1 that we almost all accept the second principle of human dignity, the principle that requires each of us to take personal responsibility for his ethical convictions, including his religious convictions. People in the religious traditions that flourish in America now accept this principle, indeed insist upon it, as among the articles of their faith. That principle, remember, does not purport to bar the influence of culture or family tradition on people's religious choice. That would be pointless. Nor does it bar achieving conviction through faith, revelation, or the direct perception of divinity unmediated by argument. It bars only subordinating ourselves to other people who aim to make and enforce deliberate choices of religious faith for us.

Religious as well as secular Americans would acknowledge that responsibility to reject subordination; faith for them must be a matter of conviction from within, not compulsion from without. So we can frame an argument around this question: can people who understand and accept that responsibility consistently hope for a religious state, even a tolerant religious state? That is a question about the best interpretation of a principle we share as common ground. In the next several pages I shall argue for one answer to that question: that the principle of personal responsibility requires a tolerant secular state and rules out a tolerant religious state. I do not suppose that my argument will persuade many who initially disagree with that claim. But I do hope that it will provoke them to explain why they believe my argument fails and then to construct a different understanding of that principle, one that supports a different conclusion from mine.

Why Religious Freedom?

If the question whether the United States should be a tolerant religious or a tolerant secular state were to be decided by asking whether a majority of Americans are religious, the verdict would go to the former. The great majority of Americans embrace some form of monotheistic religious faith; the great bulk of them are Christians. But I am now assuming that the great bulk of Americans also accept the principle of personal responsibility I described. People who self-consciously accept that principle insist on the freedom they need to exercise that responsibility; they insist on legal rights to protect that freedom. The right of religious freedom that both of our models recognize is such a right; it protects people's responsibility to find value in their lives. But as I said, the models differ in how broadly they interpret the right of religious freedom and in their attitude toward state establishment of religion. Which of these interpretations better matches what the principle of personal responsibility requires in a community of mostly religious citizens?

We must talk about liberty, and I must first clarify my vocabulary. I shall use the word "liberty" to describe the set of rights that government should establish and enforce to protect people's personal ethical responsibility properly understood. I shall use the word "freedom" in a more neutral way, so that any time the government prevents someone from acting as he might wish, it limits his freedom. Defined in that way, freedom is not a political value. There is nothing to regret when I am prevented from kidnapping your children—no wrong has been done to me, even one that might be deemed necessary or excusable. But liberty defined as I defined it is of course a political value; it identifies those areas of freedom that government does do wrong to limit or invade. That is the value we must now explore.

The two models we are contrasting disagree in the scope and range of the religious freedom each offers. The tolerant religious model supposes a narrow conception of religious freedom that does not include, for instance, a right to choose abortion or to marry someone of the same sex. The tolerant secular model insists on a broader conception that does include the right to make such choices. These are competing theories of liberty. Which theory is more appropriate for a nation in which a large majority believes in a god?

I said earlier that supporters of the tolerant religious model might defend their narrow conception of religious freedom by insisting that religion is special and therefore needs a distinct kind of protection that does not apply to other activities. In fact, however, on a more careful look, that defense is not available to them because they extend religious freedom to atheists as well as believers, and they need a more general theory of liberty to defend that extension. The statesmen who founded the American nation in the eighteenth century had very practical reasons for protecting religious dissent. That story is familiar: the terrible religious wars in Europe in the sixteenth and seventeenth centuries demonstrated the tragic consequences of imposed religious orthodoxy, and religious freedom was the best and perhaps only means to stop civil war and slaughter. Our founders were particularly conscious of religion's bloody history: religious dissent was not only instrumental in settling several American colonies but a source of division and even violence within them. But that explanation will not serve as a justification for tolerating atheism or even marginal religions now. Political stability is much greater in contemporary America and in other mature democracies than it was in seventeenth-century Europe. We might provoke a horrific wave of terrorism if we outlawed Islam in America, but we would have little to fear in denying churches or assembly to Jehovah's Witnesses or the disciples of the Reverend Moon, and even less to fear if we required the children of atheists to stand and recite the Lord's Prayer in school.

In any case, however, people drawn to the tolerant religious model think that religious freedom for everyone, including atheists, is a matter of principle, not simply wise policy. Some of them think that that freedom is itself a matter of theological requirement; John Locke, for example, held that a forced conversion was of no use to God, and the Virginia Bill for Religious Liberty, the precursor of the religion clauses of the First Amendment, stated that all attempts to coerce religion "are a departure from the plan of the Holy author of our religion." But even if most religious Americans hold that view, this would not explain why they think it wrong for the government to establish churches and give them financial support as other nations do. It might be said, finally, that religion is special and needs special protection for a different reason: for many people religious observance is a matter of transcendent importance touching, as they believe it does, their eternal salvation or damnation so that any constraint on religious practice would do particularly grave damage to them. But of course atheists believe no such thing.

So once we consider the details of the tolerant religious view as this is now defended in America, we see that it must rely on a more general theory of liberty to explain why it is as tolerant as it is. It cannot simply appeal to the importance or value of religion to defend that level of tolerance. This is an important conclusion because it means that the argument between the two models must be conducted on a more general philosophical plane. If each of the two approaches must appeal to some more general conception of liberty, we may be able to clarify the argument between them by considering the philosophical question of what liberty really is.

The Structure of Liberty

As I said, liberty is not just freedom. No one has a right to live precisely as he wishes; no one has a right to a life dedicated to violence, theft, cruelty, or murder. Government limits people's freedom not only to protect the safety and freedom of other people but in many other ways as well. Taxes also limit my power to live as I wish; I can put more of what I believe to be valuable into my life if the government allows me to fill my purse and keep it filled. But we do not, at least most of us, count taxation as a constraint on liberty. Sometimes paying taxes does seem an insult to self-respect; it seemed that way to Henry David Thoreau, for example, because he objected strongly to how his taxes would be used. But most of us, most of the time, do not regard paying taxes as an indignity or an insult to our power to choose our own values. How shall we clarify the basic principle of personal responsibility and the liberty it requires so as to recognize these important limits to the right to live according to one's preferred values?

I propose this initial formulation: *liberty is the right to do what you want with the resources that are rightfully yours.*[15] I must decide what is rightfully mine before I can claim a right to shape my own life in any particular way. I cannot claim a right to live like Attila the Hun on a bad day, because I cannot think that your life and property are at my disposal. If we accept this account of liberty, then we must also accept that liberty is not damaged when government restricts freedom if it has a plausible *distributive* reason for doing so. A distributive justification appeals to some theory about the fair allocation of the resources and opportunities that are available to the community as a whole. Laws prohibiting damage to person or property are distributive because they assume a theory of property and respect for property. That is a distributive matter. Tax laws are also distributive because they assume some theory about who should bear and in what proportion the costs of society, including the costs of remedying the injustice of an unregulated market economy. Of course a regulation cannot be justified as distributive if its putative distributive justification is unsound. Unfair taxation does compromise liberty, but fair taxation does not.

This conception of liberty supposes that people have a right to choose and live their values only within the space allowed by proper distributional regulations and constraints of these different kinds. That follows from the important constraint I mentioned in chapter 1: if we accept the two principles of human dignity, we must work out the implications of each in the light of the other. If I accept both that everyone's life is of equal intrinsic value and that everyone has the same personal responsibility for his life as I do, then these assumptions must shape my definition of my own responsibility. I must define that responsibility so that it is compatible with a like responsibility among other people because their lives are of equal importance to mine. So I cannot regard proper distributional constraints, which allocate resources among these different lives, as compromising my personal responsibility for my own life. I must regard them as helping to define what my personal responsibility is.

But we must now distinguish distributive justifications for constraints on people's freedom, which are in principle acceptable, from other kinds of justification that might be proposed. A *personally judgmental* justification appeals to or presupposes a theory about what kinds of lives are intrinsically good or bad for the people who lead those lives. Any justification for making sodomy illegal that cites the immorality or baseness of that sexual practice is personally judgmental. Personally judgmental justifications must in turn be distinguished from *impersonally judgmental* justifications that appeal to the intrinsic value of some impersonal object or state of affairs rather than to the intrinsic value of certain kinds of lives. If government limits the freedom of timber companies in order to protect great forests, it appeals to the impersonally judgmental justification that such forests are natural treasures.

The principle of personal responsibility distinguishes between these two kinds of judgmental justifications because it insists only that people have responsibility for their own ethical values, that is, their own convictions about why their life has intrinsic importance and what kind of life would best realize that value for them. It does not give them an immunity from laws that protect impersonal values like natural or artistic treasures. So government does not offend that principle when it adopts zoning schemes to protect the architectural or historic integrity of some part of a city, for example, or when it uses public funds collected in taxes to support museums. Of course not every impersonally judgmental justification is acceptable; no one's freedom should be curtailed just to protect a worthless architectural style or an undistinguished clump of trees. Impersonally judgmental justifications must also respect proper distributional principles: government should choose methods for protecting resources that distribute the burden of the protection fairly. Preserving the architectural integrity of some neighborhood through conservation zoning, for instance, is normally legitimate only if it leaves opportunity for radical architectural expression somewhere else.

This distinction between personally and impersonally judgmental justifications for limiting freedom is crucial to the defense of liberty. We must distinguish between laws that violate dignity by usurping an individual's responsibility for his own ethical values and those that exercise a community's essential collective responsibility to identify and protect nonethical values. We may leave religious and other ethical values to individual judgment and conscience, but we can only protect our aesthetic environment together. However, this indispensable distinction is elusive in some cases. The Supreme Court has tried to draw it on several occasions. It had once to decide whether an atheist who believes that all war is wrong has the kind of "religious" conviction that entitles him to conscientious objector status. The Court ruled that this depends on whether the atheist's conviction has "a place in the life of its possessor parallel to that filled by the orthodox belief in God of one who clearly qualifies for the exemption."[16] In the Court's *Casey* decision, in which it reaffirmed its *Roe v. Wade* holding that states may not criminalize early abortion, three justices tried to capture the distinction between ethical and other values in a different way. "[A]t the heart of liberty," they said, "is the right to define one's own concept of existence, of meaning, of the universe, and of the mystery of human life."[17] They added that beliefs about such matters "define the attributes of personhood." Decisions about abortion, they held, are decisions of that character, and freedom therefore requires that the final decision about abortion before viability must be left to a pregnant woman and her doctor. The Supreme Court relied on that language in a later case of great importance: *Lawrence v. Texas*, in which it held that laws purporting to make all homosexual sodomy a crime are also unconstitutional; it decided that sexual orientation and activity are also a matter of ethical value rather than some other form of value.[18] In these various decisions and opinions, the justices tried to identify the convictions that define "personhood," the convictions through which a person tries to identify the value and point of human life and the relationships, achievements, and experiences that would realize that value in his own life.

Orthodox religious convictions are plainly in that category, and so are people's convictions about the role and direction of love, intimacy, and sexuality in their lives. These beliefs and commitments fix the meaning and tone of the most important associations people form; they are drawn from and feed back into their more general philosophical beliefs about the character and value of human life. But a logging executive's conviction that ancient forests are of no particular interest or value—that (as an American vice president once put it) if you've seen one tree, you've seen them all—is not an ethical conviction. It is neither derived from nor formative of convictions about the importance of human life or of achievement in a human life. No doubt we can think of more troublesome cases in which it is less clear to which of these categories some belief or conviction belongs. The decisions of constitutional courts charged with enforcing the distinction between these categories are sometimes difficult. But the distinction is nevertheless crucial, and in the most important cases—about religion, family, and sex, for instance—it is not difficult to draw.

Liberty and Culture

We have now identified the main structural features of a conception of liberty that respects the principles of human dignity. Liberty is not infringed by constraints that can be justified on sound distributive or sound impersonally judgmental grounds. My liberty is not compromised when I am taxed to fund a new road to the hospital or when I am forbidden to build a postmodern house in a Georgian block. But it is compromised by coercive laws that can be justified only on personally judgmental grounds. We may allow that some personally judgmental constraints are permissible; these are the superficially paternalistic constraints of seat belts and pharmaceutical regulation. These do not, on a second look, offend the principle of personal responsibility because they are based on plausible assumptions about what the people's values actually are and also because they are typically supported by important distributive justifications. But some laws can be justified only on deep paternalistic assumptions—that the majority knows better than some individuals where value in their lives is to be found and that it is entitled to force those individuals to find it there. These laws are offensive to liberty and must be condemned as affronts to people's personal responsibility for their own lives.

Now these important conclusions may strike you as decisive in the choice between our two models of religion and politics, decisive for a tolerant secular state and against a tolerant religious state. But that assumption is premature because the important argument has just begun. The strongest and most popular case for a religious state in a nation most of whose members are religious is not paternalistic but cultural. That case rests on the assumption that a political majority has a right to create the culture it wants to live in and raise its children in not for the sake of the minority who might protest but for their own sakes—because a society openly committed to religious values is better for them. Compare, for a moment, the arguments that are now deemed the best arguments for the prohibition or regulation of pornography. Censorship of pornography was once defended on paternalistic grounds: pornography corrupts those who read it, and prohibition is therefore good for them. But now a different justification for censorship is much more popular: sexually explicit material should be prohibited in order to protect the culture in which all citizens must live. Parents will have an easier time teaching their children a proper appreciation of sex as intimacy constructed by love if those children are not constantly exposed to materials that offer a very different and less attractive picture. Moreover, children are not the only people threatened by a debasement of sex in the culture. Women in particular are insulted and their subordination reinforced by their depiction as sexual slaves or masochists in much of pornography. Indeed, everyone, men and women alike, may find their lives cheapened by the sordid commercial exploitation of life's most intimate experiences. That is not a paternalistic argument. It cites instead the right of a majority to shape the culture that has powerful consequences for its own lives.

This is the crucial issue we must now face about religion. Who should have control, and in what way, over the moral, ethical, and aesthetic culture in which we must all live? This complex culture is shaped by many forces, but I now isolate two of these. It is shaped by discrete decisions of individual people about what to produce and what to buy and at what price, about what to read and say, about what to wear, what music to listen to, and what god, if any, to pray to. Our culture is in large part a vector of many millions of such decisions that people make, as individuals, one by one, every day. But our culture is also shaped by law, that is, by collective decisions taken by elected legislators as to how we must all behave. Interest-rate policy fixed by the Federal Reserve Board shapes our economic culture, zoning ordinances shape our aesthetic culture, and civil rights laws shape our moral culture. How shall we decide which aspects of culture should be influenced collectively in that way and which should be left to the organic process of individual decision?

Americans who feel entitled to a tolerant religious society assume that a majority of citizens has the right, acting through the normal political process, to shape the religious character of our shared culture by law. They accept that the majority must also respect the right of dissenters to their own religious observance or to none. But they insist that if the majority thinks that religious faith is good for a community, it can direct the power and prestige of the state to endorse that faith, deploy the finances and authority of compulsory public education to promote it, and shape the emotional charge of patriotic celebration to affirm it. That is the explicit claim of the religious Right now.

Newt Gingrich proclaims that 92 percent of Americans "believe in God" and quotes with pleasure the 1931 Supreme Court decision I mentioned that announced, "We are a Christian people."[19] The majority, in his view, has a right to the culture it prefers, and the courts that try to drive any god from public life cheat the majority of that right. President Bush has become enamored of the phrase "culture of life," and that phrase was on the lips of many conservatives throughout the tragic long death of Terri Schiavo. The phrase is code for the culture that conservatives hope to create not through individual choice but through legal compulsion. The secular model insists, on the contrary, that our collective religious culture should be created not through the collective power of the state but organically, through the separate acts of conviction, commitment, and faith of people drawn to such acts. That is finally the most important contrast between the two models, the true contrast between the ideals of public faith and private conviction. Which view best matches our shared ideals of human dignity?

The second principle of dignity assigns each of us a responsibility to assess and choose ethical values for himself rather than to yield to the coercive choices of others. Our culture of course influences our choice of values; our personalities are in that way all partly constructed out of the millions of choices that others have made for themselves. Their choices largely determine the books we read, the images we see, and the expectations that shape what we instinctively do. The second principle does not forbid this inevitable influence; it forbids subordination, which is something very different. It forbids my accepting that other people have the right to dictate what I am to think about what makes a good life or to forbid me to act as I wish because they think my ethical values are wrong. It therefore forbids me to accept any manipulation of my culture that is both collective and deliberate—that deploys the collective power and treasure of the community as a whole and that aims to affect the ethical choices and values of its members. That is subordination. It makes no difference that the purpose of such manipulation is to benefit the manipulators. I must reject manipulation even if the values it is designed to protect or instill are my own values because my dignity is as much outraged by coercion intended to freeze my values as by coercion intended to change them.

Of course a majority may adopt coercive policies that are justified on distributive grounds of justice or impersonally judgmental grounds of conservation even when these policies are likely to affect how people conceive of successful lives. Redistributive taxation and civil rights acts, for example, may well transform the culture in ways that will affect citizens' sense of how they can and should live. Such measures impact our ethical culture, perhaps strongly, but they can be justified entirely apart from any assumption that that impact will be ethically beneficial, that people will lead better as well as fairer lives in a culture so transformed.

So I can accept coercive policies of that sort without any sense that I have abandoned to others my responsibility to decide for myself what ethical values my life should reflect. It is different when people in power use that power deliberately to shape an ethical culture more suited to their tastes. I cannot accept their right to do that without conceding that a majority has the power to shape my convictions according to its standards of how to live well.

It is worth noticing that Americans are unwilling to grant political majorities a parallel collective power over the fundamentals of our economic culture. Socialist societies do give people in power the authority to shape the economic environment for everyone by stipulating price and the allocation of resource and production. But we insist on a free market in goods and services; we insist, that is, that the economic culture be shaped by a vector of individual decisions reflecting individual values and wishes. Yes, distributive fairness requires that our free market be structured to protect against externalities of different kinds, and to protect people who for other reasons will not be treated fairly by pure market allocation. I discuss these required market structures and constraints in chapter 4. But an acceptable market regulation must take some form that does not deprive any group or person of an impact on supply and price that reflects its or his own wishes and values. Economic socialism is an insult to liberty as well as to efficiency, and that is a view most enthusiastically held by the conservatives who favor a religious model for noneconomic culture. They do not realize that liberty is even more perilously at stake in the religious than in the economic case.

So the judgment made by officials who decide that the state should express religious values in order to promote a culture of religion is just as personally judgmental and just as offensive to liberty as a paternalistic justification would be. It makes no difference that a large majority may hope for a religious culture. People's personal responsibility for their own lives is as much frustrated by allowing a majority of citizens to impose their values on everyone through legislation as it would be by allowing some minority to do that.

Issues

Science and Religion

The conception of liberty we constructed, which forbids coercion justified on personally judgmental grounds, does indeed favor the tolerant secular over the tolerant religious model of government even in a community most of whose members are religious. That, in any case, is the burden of the argument I have now offered you. I hope that those who disagree will respond by offering reasons for thinking my argument wrong. They might, for example, reject the general account I gave of liberty and of the importance I placed on the distinction between personally judgmental reasons for influencing culture, on the one hand, and distributive and impersonally judgmental reasons, on the other. But any contrary argument they might produce must be grounded in a theory of liberty of comparable scope, and if they do accept the principle of personal responsibility, their theory of liberty must be drawn from and fit that principle. It would not do simply to think that because my argument justifies conclusions they dislike it must be wrong.

I will not try to anticipate such rival arguments. Instead I shall fill out my own argument by returning to some of the specific issues that I said divide the two models as they divide the two cultures, liberal and conservative, blue and red, into which the nation is now supposedly divided. The politically most consequential of these issues remains abortion. Many conservatives say that abortion is murder, and the fervor of their opposition—some conservatives have killed doctors who perform abortions—testifies to that belief. A political community must somehow decide collectively, through courts or legislatures, whether abortion is murder; if it is, then outlawing abortion is necessary on distributive rather than judgmental grounds and constitutes no offense to liberty. If abortion is not murder, however, then it can be said to be wrong only on personally judgmental grounds, which a society dedicated to liberty must avoid. Whether abortion is murder does not depend, in my view, on whether a fetus is a human being at some very early point after conception—of course it is—but on whether it has interests and so rights to protect those interests at that early stage.

I have argued, elsewhere, that it does not.[20] No creature has interests who has not had a mental life that has generated those interests.[21] It makes sense to say that people who are now dead or permanently unconscious still have interests. We mean that their lives will have been more successful if the interests they formed while alive and conscious flourish when they are unconscious or dead.[22] My life will have gone better if, as I very much hope, my family prospers after my death, for instance. But creatures who have never felt pain or made plans or formed attachments of any kind have developed no interests to fulfill or frustrate. So I do not believe that early fetuses have rights or that abortion is murder, and I therefore believe the Supreme Court was right to hold that making early abortion a crime is inconsistent with respecting personal responsibility. But my argument is too complex to repeat now, so I simply refer those who are interested to my book on the subject and turn instead to a closely related issue that does not raise any question of murder.

This is the question of science. Nothing frightens liberals and moderates more, I think, than the vision of religious organizations and movements dictating what may be taught to children in public schools either through formal legislation or school board rulings or through informal intimidation of teachers. Many Americans are horrified by the prospect of a new dark age imposed by militant superstition; they fear a black, know-nothing night of ignorance in which America becomes an intellectually backward and stagnant theocracy. But someone must decide what children are taught about history and science. If the elected school board or the majority of parents in a particular jurisdiction sincerely believes that Darwin's theory of evolution is radically wrong, why should they not have the power to prevent that error from being taught to their children, just as they have the power to prevent teachers from converting their classes to the Flat Earth Society? It is no answer that children must not be taught the biblical theory of creation because the Bible must be kept out of the classroom. The Bible also condemns murder, but that does not mean that children cannot be taught that murder is wrong.

But the cosmological and biological beliefs of the religious conservatives do not just coincide with their religious convictions; they would reject those cosmological and biological beliefs out of hand if these were *not* dictated by those religious convictions. Almost all religious conservatives accept that the methods of empirical science are in general well designed for the discovery of truth and that their children must be taught the reliability of those methods if they are to be prepared for their adult lives. They would not countenance requiring or permitting teachers to teach, even as an alternative theory, what science has established as unquestionably and beyond challenge false: that the sun orbits the Earth or that radioactivity is harmless, for example. The biblical account of the creation of the universe and of human beings is just as silly from the perspective of any scientific discipline. Some religious people find that for them faith trumps science in these and the other few remaining areas in which faith challenges science. They deny the truth of Darwinian theory in the self-conscious exercise of their personal responsibility to fix the role of faith in their lives. That is their right; it would be a terrible violation of liberty to try to coerce them out of that conviction. But if they are to respect the second principle of human dignity that we have been exploring, they must not try to impose that faith on others, including children who are coerced into public education.

In recent years a few religious scientists have claimed a refutation of the main tenets of Darwinian evolution that does not rely on biblical authority or the biblical young-Earth account of creation. This refutation purports only to show that an "intelligent design" rather than the unguided processes of nature and natural selection that Darwin postulated must be responsible for creating life and human beings. The thesis has quickly gained enormous attention and notoriety. Several states have considered requiring teachers to describe the intelligent design theory as an available alternative to standard evolutionary theory in public high school biology classes. A Pennsylvania school board adopted that requirement a few years ago, and though a federal judge then struck the proposal down as an unconstitutional imposition of Christian doctrine in public schools,[23] other public bodies in other states are still pursuing similar programs. President Bush recently appeared to endorse these campaigns; he said, "I felt like both sides ought to be properly taught."[24] The Senate majority leader, Senator Frist, who is said to covet the Republican nomination for the presidency in 2008, agreed. He said that teaching intelligent design theory along with evolution, as competing scientific explanations of the creation of human life, is fair because it "doesn't force any particular theory on anyone."[25]

If there is any scientific evidence against evolution, then of course students should be taught what it is. But the intelligent design movement has discovered no scientific evidence at all. We must distinguish the following three claims: (1) Scientists have not yet shown to all their satisfaction how the Darwinian processes of random mutation and natural selection explain every feature of the development of plant and animal life on our planet; some features remain areas of speculation and controversy among them. (2) There is now good scientific evidence that these features cannot be explained within the general Darwinian structure; a successful explanation will therefore require abandoning that structure altogether. (3) This evidence also at least suggests that an intelligent designer created life and designed the processes of development that have produced human beings.

The first of these claims is both correct and unsurprising. The details of evolutionary theory, like the phenomena it tries to explain, are massively complex. Eminent biologists disagree in heated arguments about, for example, whether some features of developed life are best explained as accidents or as byproducts of no survival value in themselves. Evolutionary biologists face other challenges and disagree in how best to meet them.

The second of the three claims is false. It does not follow from the fact that evolutionary scientists have not yet found or agreed on a solution to some puzzle that their methods have been shown to be defective, any more than it follows from historical controversies or unproved mathematical conjectures that the methods of historians or mathematicians must be abandoned. Scientists have so far found no reason to doubt that evolutionary puzzles can be solved within the general apparatus of Darwinian theory; none of the rival solutions they offer calls that general apparatus into question. The proponents of intelligent design theory claim in their lectures, popular writing, and television appearances that the irreducible complexity of certain forms of life—no element of even certain primitive forms of life could be removed without making it impossible for that form of life to survive—proves that Darwin's theory must be rejected root and branch. But their arguments are very bad, a judgment confirmed by their failure so far to expose these arguments to professionals by submitting articles to peer-reviewed journals.[26] It is no explanation of this failure to suppose that the scientific establishment would reject even well-reasoned articles that challenged Darwin. On the contrary, a scientifically sound general attack on evolution would be very exciting news indeed; a Nobel Prize might be around the corner.

The third claim would be false even if the second claim were true. If the failure to find a natural physical or biological explanation of some physical or biological phenomenon were taken to be evidence of divine intervention, which could then be accepted as the phenomenon's cause, science would disappear for at least two reasons. First, science depends on the possibility of verification or falsification, and there can be no evidence that a superhuman power that is unconstrained by natural laws either has or has not caused anything at all. Second, once divine intervention is accepted as a candidate for the explanation of any natural event, it must be acknowledged always to be available as an explanation of everything for which no conventional scientific explanation has yet been discovered. Doctors have established a strong correlation between cigarette smoking and lung cancer, but they do not yet know the mechanisms through which one causes the other. Why should we not then say that an explanation is nevertheless at hand: God punishes select cigarette smokers? Indeed, once divine intervention is accepted as a possible candidate for scientific explanation, it is available even as a rival to a fully adequate conventional explanation. Why should we prefer a physicist's account of global warming, which suggests that the process will continue unless and until people reduce the level of their carbon pollution of the atmospheres, to the rival account that a god is warming the planet for his own unknown purposes and will cool it again when he wishes? Once we accept any miracle of creation, then we must accept that both divine and conventional scientific explanations fit any set of facts equally well. Very few socially conservative Americans would vote for a school board that allowed teachers to explain anything they wished by citing a miracle. The concept of intelligent design appeals to some of them because it purports to give scientific blessing to exactly and only the specific miracle on which they believe their religion rests: creation. But that discrimination cannot be sustained; once miracles are recognized as competitive with scientific explanations, the damage to reason cannot be limited or controlled.

I am not now denying the truth of any theological hypothesis; I am not denying that those many millions of people who believe that a god created the universe or life or human beings are right. But their belief, even if it is in some way warranted, does not provide a scientific explanation of those events. This distinction is not merely semantic; I am not quibbling about the meaning of "science." If we are to protect dignity by protecting people's responsibility for their own personal values, then we must build our compulsory education and our collective endorsements of truth around the distinction between faith and reason. We need a defensible conception of science not only for the intensely practical reason that we must prepare our children and youth to advance knowledge and to compete in the world's economy, but also to protect the personal responsibility of our citizens for their religious faith. We need an account of science, in our public philosophy of government, that does not make its authority depend on commitment to any set of religious or ethical values. So Senator Frist made a serious mistake when he said that describing intelligent design only as a scientific alternative to evolution doesn't "force any theory on anyone." In fact, it damages young students, practically and politically, by using the state's authority to force on them a false and disabling view of what science is.

When President Bush said that intelligent design should be taught in the schools, his science adviser, John Marburger, said that "Darwinian theory is a cornerstone of modern biology," and that Bush meant only that "students should be taught that some people have suggested that Intelligent Design is a viable alternative theory."[27] If so, we should welcome Bush's suggestion. In chapter 5 I describe a contemporary Political Controversy course that I believe should be a standard part of high school curriculums in the United States. The intelligent design movement should be studied and assessed in that course, at least until it is replaced by some other religious antievolution movement. It should not, however, be tolerated in the biology classroom.

Allegiance and Ceremony

Now consider another issue of contemporary controversy: the American pledge of allegiance. This is the official pledge of political fidelity that by tradition is recited in schools and on some ceremonial occasions. For some decades the ritual pledge has included, by act of Congress, a reasonably ecumenical religious declaration: the pledge recites that America is "one nation under God." The pledge is voluntary; the Supreme Court held long ago, even before this reference to God was made part of the pledge, that schoolchildren could not be forced to recite it. People drawn to the tolerant religious model support the religious reference in the official pledge because they believe it both symbolizes and achieves an indispensable fusion of religion and patriotism. They point out that since no one is required to recite the official pledge, no one is forced into an act that contradicts his conscience. They might acknowledge that an American who stands silent while the crowd around him recites the pledge is made to feel an outsider. That is nevertheless his choice, however; if he cannot subscribe to an ecumenical endorsement of monotheism, he *is* an outsider, and there can be harm in reminding him and everyone else of that fact.

But dignity does not simply command that no one be forced to recite what he does not believe. It assigns us a positive responsibility to choose ethical values for ourselves, and though, as I said, we know we are influenced by a thousand dimensions of culture in making those choices, we must nevertheless refuse to accept subordination to a government that deliberately and coercively manipulates our choices. There can be no distributive justification for creating an official pledge that makes full citizens feel like outsiders. There can be only a personally judgmental justification: deliberately influencing the shared culture to associate religion and patriotism, on the ground that that association is desirable, in a way that makes it more difficult for someone who wishes to embrace patriotism free of religion to do so. It is plainly part of people's responsibility for their own values to define for themselves the religious or metaphysical assumptions of political allegiance. The coercive impact of an officially endorsed ritual is no more acceptable than the open manipulation of compelled assertion.

That coercive impact is in fact not very strong, however, and so though the official pledge is a violation of liberty, it is not a practically serious one. Just as an atheist can fish in his pocket for a coin that bears a message of trust in God or stand at the opening ceremony of prayer in congressional or court sessions without any sense of self-betrayal, so he can mouth the words of the pledge without loss of integrity. Few children treat the detailed wording of the pledge they recite in school as having the authority even of the solemn vows they make in the playground. But that means only that the intended purpose of making the pledge theological has failed, not that that purpose is in itself legitimate.

There is, in my view, even less reason for concern about a subject that has much occupied the federal courts: public displays of ceremonial icons that have a religious heritage and association but that also play a nonreligious civic role as centerpieces of festivity. It is true that public Christmas trees are bought with taxes collected from nonbelievers, but the expense is trivial. It would be wrong for a community to recognize the great occasions of only one of the religions of its members, which explains why Christmas trees are now often flanked by menorahs and no doubt, when suitable, crescents as well. Equality of concern and respect for citizens is an independent requirement. But, as the Supreme Court has come to recognize in a series of awkward opinions, there is precious little endorsement of religion in these public displays, and nonbelievers can comfortably enjoy their secular significance with no more sense of inauthenticity than they feel when they spend a quarter.

Marriage

My final example—gay marriage—is a very different matter. The institution of marriage is unique; it is a distinct mode of association and commitment that carries centuries and volumes of social and personal meaning. We can no more create an alternative mode of commitment carrying a parallel intensity of meaning than we can create a substitute for poetry or for love. The status of marriage is therefore a social resource of irreplaceable value to those to whom it is offered; it enables two people together to create value in their lives that they could not create if that institution had never existed. We know that people of the same sex often love one another with the same passion as people of different sexes do. If we allow a heterosexual couple access to that wonderful resource but deny it to a homosexual couple, we make it possible for one pair but not the other to realize what they both believe to be an important value in their lives. By what right may society discriminate in that way?

Since we accept the principle of personal responsibility and recognize the rights that it entails, we need a particularly compelling justification, which must not be a personally judgmental justification, for a discrimination of that magnitude. The opponents of gay marriage who have tried to furnish a nonjudgmental justification have had to resort to thoroughly speculative hypotheses. The judges who dissented in the Massachusetts Supreme Court from that court's recognition of gay marriage suggested that a ban might be justified because a heterosexual marriage provides a better background than homosexual unions for raising children. There is no good, let alone compelling, evidence for that opinion, however. The perception itself reflects a judgmental religious perspective, and it is anyway belied by the practice, in Massachusetts as well as other states, of permitting unmarried same-sex couples to adopt children.

There is an even more popular justification: that society does not discriminate against homosexuals if it forbids same-sex marriages but creates same-sex civil unions that provide most or all of the material advantages of marriage. That argument refutes itself. If there is no difference between the material and legal consequences of marriage or a contrived civil union, then why should marriage be reserved for heterosexuals? That can be only because marriage has a spiritual dimension that civil union does not. This may be a religious dimension, which some same-sex couples want as much as heterosexuals do. Or it may be the resonance of history and culture that I described and that both kinds of couples covet. But whatever it is, if there are reasons for withholding the status from gay couples, then these must also be reasons why civil union is not an equivalent opportunity.

The only genuine argument against gay marriage—the argument that actually generates such fierce opposition to it—has the same form as the argument for a religious pledge of allegiance, but the stakes are of course very much higher. The case against gay marriage, put most sympathetically, comes to this: the institution of marriage is, as I said, a unique and immensely valuable cultural resource. Its meaning and hence its value have accreted organically over centuries, and the assumption that marriage is the union of a man and a woman is so embedded in its meaning that it would become a different institution, and hence a less valuable institution, were that assumption now challenged and lost. Just as we might struggle to maintain the meaning and value of any other great natural or artistic resource, so we should struggle to retain this uniquely valuable cultural resource.

That argument captures the appeal of the opposition to gay marriage, but it must be rejected because, as I hope is now clear, it contradicts the premise of our shared ideals of liberty and the personal responsibility that liberty protects. This becomes dramatically clear when we substitute "religion" for "marriage" in the argument I just constructed. Everything I said about the cultural heritage and value of marriage is equally true of the general institution of religion: religion is an irreplaceable cultural resource in which billions of people find immense and incomparable value. Its meaning, like that of marriage, has accreted over a great many centuries. But its meaning, again like that of marriage, is subject to quite dramatic change through organic processes as new religions and sects develop and as new threats to established doctrine and practice are generated by secular developments in science, politics, or theories of social justice. People's sense of what religion is has been altered, in recent decades, by the feminist movement, for instance, which demands women priests, by the rise and fall in popular imagination of various forms of mysticism, hallucinogenic experimentation, pantheism, Unitarianism, fundamentalist doctrines, radical liberation movements, and by a thousand other shifts in religious impulse that began in individual decision and ended in seismic changes in what religion can and does mean. American religious conservatives, even those who regard themselves as evangelical, do not imagine that the cultural meaning of religion should be frozen by laws prohibiting people with new visions from access to the title, legal status, or tax and economic benefits of religious organization.

The cultural argument against gay marriage I described is therefore inconsistent with the instincts and insight we almost all share and that I suggest are captured in the second principle of human dignity. The argument supposes that the culture that shapes our values is the property only of some of us—those who happen to enjoy political power for the moment—to sculpt and protect in the shape we admire. That is a deep mistake; in a genuinely free society, the world of ideas and values belongs to no one and to everyone. Who will argue—not just declare—that I am wrong?

CHAPTER 4

TAXES AND LEGITIMACY

Tax and Spend

SO FAR, I HAVE discussed two of the most dramatic issues that seem to divide Americans into rival cultural camps, conservative and liberal or, if you prefer, red and blue. May we ignore the traditional rights of our own domestic criminal process in confronting the terrorist threat? What role should religion play in our politics, our government, and our public life? Now we take up a third issue that is equally divisive and has more consequence than either of those two for the day-to-day lives of almost all our citizens: taxes.

In his first term, President Bush engineered very dramatic tax reductions, even more dramatic because they took effect during a very expensive military campaign. By 2005, Congress, at his behest, had reduced taxes by $1.8 trillion over ten years, and these tax reductions had favored the richest Americans. In that year Bush and Republican leaders of Congress proposed further tax cuts and also proposed to make the tax cuts already achieved permanent. Hurricane Katrina, which devastated New Orleans and other parts of the Gulf states, shocked America because the government's tardy and ineffective response suggested a lack of concern for the poor residents of those areas, most of them black, whose lives had been ruined. This political reaction, and also the growing distaste of some moderate Republicans for further tax cuts while the government was cutting social programs to help pay for the reconstruction of the Gulf area, forced the Republican leadership to postpone, at least, these further tax cuts. "Obviously, the juxtaposition of cutting taxes and food stamps within a few days is not attractive," said James T. Walsh, a Republican congressman from New York.[1] But the president continues to call for the further tax cuts he believes desirable.

The distribution of wealth and income in the United States is striking. In 2001, 1 percent of our population owned more than a third of our wealth, the top 10 percent of the population owned 70 percent of it, and the bottom 50 percent only 2.8 percent.[2] In 2001, according to United States Census Bureau figures, the top 20 percent in income earned more than 50 percent of aggregate income, and the top 5 percent earned more than 22 percent.[3] In 2004, according to a report by the Institute for Policy Studies, the average chief executive in large companies earned 431 times as much as the average worker in those companies.[4]

Bush's tax cuts have made the great gap between rich and poor even greater. The Brookings Institution Tax Policy Center calculated that more than half of the benefits of one provision—exempting corporate dividends from income tax—would flow to the top 5 percent of the population. This tax reduction gave each person with an income of over a million dollars a year on average more than five hundred times the benefit it gave each person with an income of under $100,000.[5]

Republican leaders say that these tax cuts for the rich were necessary to stimulate the economy. But Bush's tax cuts have converted a multitrillion-dollar surplus, which he inherited, into an unprecedented and dangerous fiscal deficit—Congress's budget agency has predicted between $3.5 and $4 trillion in the next decade—without helping the overall economy much, if at all.[6] The improvements in the economy since 2001 have benefited, once again, mainly the rich; median household income since then has actually fallen,[7] and the average income of American families fell by 2.3 percent in 2004.[8] As the president's own Council of Economic Advisers predicted, the tax cuts have contributed minimally to job growth.[9] In fact, as the *New York Times* reported,

> Job growth during the Bush-era recovery has been worse, by far, than in any comparable economic upturn since the 1960's. It would take some 500,000 new jobs a month every month this year just to equal the second worst job-creation record in the modern era. And while working Americans are laboring harder, hourly wages and weekly salaries—the financial lifeblood of most Americans—have been flat or falling, after inflation, since the middle of 2003.[10]

In 2002 Joseph Stiglitz, a Nobel Prize–winning economist, said, "If I were making a list of tax cuts to stimulate the economy, [Bush's] dividend tax cut would not make the short list."[11]

The political battle over taxes is not primarily a matter of economic forecasts, however. Many conservatives want taxes to be lower because they wish to reduce or eliminate the welfare programs that taxes make possible. Over the last seven decades or so—since the Roosevelt presidency brought what we call the New Deal—people in the successful democracies have largely come to accept that it is part of government's role to provide a fairer distribution of their nation's wealth than a free market economy achieves unaided. Taxes are the principal mechanism through which government plays this redistributive role. It collects money in taxes at progressive rates so that the rich pay a higher percentage of their income or wealth than the poor, and it uses the money it collects to finance a variety of programs that provide unemployment and retirement benefits, health care, aid to children in poverty, food supplements, subsidized housing, and other benefits.

Conservatives believe that this role of government should be reduced and that tax reductions are an appropriate means to that goal because, they think, taxation at even its present level is unfair to those who work hard for their income and who make possible a vibrant economy that benefits everyone. They believe that successful entrepreneurs have contributed most of all through their skill and investment courage and should not be penalized with high taxes for their success. They do not think it unfair that the rich have received the lion's share of Bush's tax cuts; they think these cuts only begin to repair the past unfairness of progressive tax rates. Liberals believe, on the contrary, that welfare provision for the poor is already much too meager in this country, and that reducing the taxes paid by the rich, which makes that provision even more meager, is deeply unfair. So the main arguments on both sides are arguments of fairness. In this chapter I hope both to deepen and to shape the disagreement by proposing a connection between tax levels and not just the fairness but the legitimacy of our government. At some point, I shall argue, government's failure to redistribute the wealth that a lightly regulated free market produces weakens government's claim to the respect and allegiance of all its citizens.

Conservatives are apparently winning the tax battle, in the United States at least. The only American presidential candidate who campaigned promising across-the-board tax raises in recent decades—Walter Mondale in 1984—lost in a landslide. George H. W. Bush asked people to watch his lips as he mouthed "No new taxes" when he won the presidency in 1988, and his subsequent defeat by Bill Clinton in 1992 is thought to be due, at least in part, to his loss of conservative support when he did, after all, raise taxes. No major-party politician proposes general tax increases now. In his 2004 campaign, John Kerry promised to raise taxes on people with incomes of $200,000 or more; Bush replied that this proposal showed that Kerry was just another "tax and spend liberal." We do not know how much that charge affected people's votes, but it is remarkable—and a contradiction of conventional political wisdom—how many people voted against what they should have seen to be in their own economic interest. Only very few people make more than $200,000 or suppose that they will. That might mean only that economic issues were swamped by either security or religious issues. But it does suggest that a great many people reject the Democrats' claim that Bush's tax policy is plainly unfair.

The argument about taxes has been characteristically shrill because, as in the case of the issues we considered in the last two chapters, it has no structure. We trade slogans. Liberals say that conservatives want to soak the poor, and conservatives say that liberals want to spend other people's money. Neither side seems able to define the level of tax it believes would be fair. So liberals complain that taxes are too low, and conservatives that they are too high, without either side being able to offer any account of how high or how low they should be and why.

I shall propose a structure for formulating contrasting answers to that question so as to make a genuine argument possible. Once again I propose to start with the principles of human dignity that I identified in chapter 1 and explored in the last two chapters. What tax policies must we pursue if we accept as foundational that human lives have intrinsic value and that each person has a personal responsibility for identifying and realizing the potential value in his own life? It is not immediately apparent what those principles do require in the area of finance, the domain of tax and spend. That is what we must now investigate.

Political Legitimacy and Equal Concern

If we accept that it is equally intrinsically important that every human life go well, then we must not treat any other human being as if his life were a matter of no great consequence. Treating him that way would demean us all, us as well as him. But—contrary to what some philosophers have suggested—that does not mean that we must always act with the same concern for everyone else's welfare as we show for ourselves and those close to us. Mostly we act with our own goals and tastes and responsibilities in mind: I may help my own children without feeling any obligation to help yours to the same degree. As individuals we owe all other human beings a *measure* of concern, but we do not owe them concern equal to that we have for ourselves, our families, and others close to us.

But the relation of a state to its members—the relation of all Americans collectively to each American separately—is a very different matter. Government must indeed show an equal concern for each of the people over whom it claims dominion. The government we elect exercises dramatic coercive power. It forces individual citizens to act in ways that we, through it, demand. We extract people's money or property through taxes, and we put them in jail or even, in our country, kill them when they do not do what we command. We not only do all this but claim a right to do it: we expect our fellow citizens to treat our collective demands as creating not just threats but moral obligations, the demanding moral obligation to obey our law. No single individual has any such power over other individuals. Our government claims all of it.

We must satisfy moral conditions before we are entitled to that authority. Not every group of people with power, even if it constitutes a majority in some population, is morally entitled to use the coercive apparatus of police and army to work its will; not every group with power can plausibly claim to impose moral obligations by fiat. What conditions must people with power meet in order to be entitled to act as governments act, so that those from whom they claim obedience are in fact morally obliged to obey? That question—of political *legitimacy*—is the oldest question of political philosophy. It has new urgency in our fragile world order when established governments are challenged and overthrown and political communities are reconfigured almost monthly. But it is also urgent even in mature and stable nations like our own when important issues of justice arise.

What test must a government meet to be legitimate? We cannot say that it is not legitimate unless it is perfectly just: that would be too strong a requirement because no existing government is perfectly just. Many political philosophers have suggested that legitimacy depends not on justice but on consent. No nation is legitimate, they say, unless its constitution enjoys the unanimous consent of those it governs. But this again is much

too strong—there are dissenters in every political community—
and philosophers have had to dilute this theory with various fic-
tions. They say that citizens give their tacit consent to the authority of a government when they remain in the territory that it
governs. But few citizens have any practical possibility of emigra-
tion, so some philosophers propose a weaker test still: they say
that a government is legitimate if its citizens would consent to its
authority under certain ideal conditions: if they were rational and
in possession of all the facts, for instance. But even that is usually
untrue. In any case, a hypothetical consent is no consent at all, so
this amendment of the theory amends the theory away.

If it would be too demanding to insist that only a perfectly just
government, or only a government all of whose citizens consent to
its authority, is legitimate, then what test should we use to decide
whether a government is legitimate? Recall the distinction I drew
in chapter 2 between political rights and human rights; the same
distinction is in point now. I emphasized the crucial difference between two questions. The first asks what a government is required
to do according to the best, most accurate understanding of the
two principles of human dignity. That is the question of citizens'
political rights, the question we should debate in our ordinary political arguments. It is the question of justice. The second asks a
different, more interpretive, question. What behavior of government would indicate that it has either not accepted the two principles as constraints on its conduct or that it is acting inconsistently
with its own understanding of what they require? That is the question of human rights, and it is also the test of political legitimacy.

A plausible theory of legitimacy must proceed without any assumption of real or hypothetical unanimous consent. It must proceed on the different assumption that when citizens are born into
a political community or join that community later, they just have
obligations to that community, including the obligation to respect
its laws whether or not they explicitly or even tacitly accept those
obligations. But they assume these political obligations only if and
so long as the community's government respects their human dignity. Only so long, that is, as it accepts the equal importance of

their lives and their personal responsibility for their own lives and tries to govern them in accordance with its sincere judgment of what those dimensions of dignity require. I can have no obligation to a community that treats me as a second-class citizen; the apartheid government of South Africa had no legitimate authority over blacks, and the governments of antebellum American states had no legitimate authority over the slaves they treated as only property.

A legitimate government must treat all those over whom it claims dominion not just with a measure of concern but with *equal* concern. I mean that it must act as if the impact of its policies on the life of any citizen is equally important. On this account political legitimacy is not an all-or-nothing matter but a matter of degree. A government elected under procedures that allow a majority of the people to replace it in due course and that by and large accepts the responsibilities of equal concern and personal responsibility may be sufficiently legitimate so that wholesale disobedience would not be justified even if some of its policies—its tax policies, for example—show an indifference to human dignity that, if it were much more general, would forfeit legitimacy altogether. South Africa could not claim any political allegiance from its black citizens because its disregard of the equal importance of their lives was total. An otherwise legitimate state whose tax policies show an isolated contempt for the poor may be morally vulnerable to a limited and targeted civil disobedience but not to revolution.

I shall be concerned with the question of legitimacy as well as of justice in the rest of this chapter. I shall ask whether our present government's economic policies have reached a plateau of indifference to the poor that shows not just an eccentric view of their rights as equal citizens but an egregious lapse in its concern for those rights. That question is of course not answered by the popularity of the government's programs. I noted in chapter 1 that many citizens who were made poorer by the Bush administration's tax cuts nevertheless voted for his reelection and continue to support his programs in polls. Some commentators suggest, as

I reported there, that these voters' cultural identification with Bush's religious values were more important to them than their economic fate under his policies.[12] Other commentators suppose that so many Americans favor tax policies that benefit the rich because they believe, on very slender evidence, that they might be rich themselves one day, that voting Republican is in that respect like buying a lottery ticket.[13] None of that matters when we are considering the legitimacy of the government's tax policies. Even if many of the poor think the government is showing them the requisite concern, others do not, and we must ask which view is right.

Nothing I have said so far about political legitimacy takes sides in any argument between conservatives and liberals, however. My account of legitimacy may be controversial as a matter of philosophy, but it is not, I hope, controversial politically. So we may now return to the subject of taxation with common ground intact. Here is our question: what tax policy must government adopt if it is to treat everyone in the political community with equal concern? If it assumes that it has the same responsibilities of care and attention toward each of its citizens?

Laissez-Faire and Small Government

We start by recognizing that just about everything the government of a large political community does—or does not do—affects the resources each of its citizens has with which to face his life. So a state cannot escape the demands of equal concern by disavowing responsibility for the economic position of any citizen. Of course, the resource that any citizen has at any given moment is a function of many variables, including his physical and mental powers and abilities, his past choices, his luck, the attitudes of others toward him, and his power or desire to produce what others want. We may call these his personal economic variables. But the upshot of all these personal variables for his actual resources and opportunities will in every case also depend on political variables: on the laws and policies of the communities in which he lives or works. We may call these laws and policies the political settlement.

The tax laws are of course an important part of the political settlement, but every other part of the law belongs to the political settlement as well: fiscal and monetary policy, labor law, environmental law and policy, urban planning, foreign policy, health care policy, transportation policy, drug and food regulation, and everything else. Changing any of these policies or laws would change the distribution of personal wealth and opportunity in the community, given the same choices, luck, attitudes, and other personal variables of each person.

So government cannot avoid the challenge of equal concern by arguing that the resources an individual has depend on his choices not the government's choices. It depends on both. The political settlement, which is under government's control, fixes the consequences for each individual for each of the sets of choices about education, training, employment, investment, production, and leisure he might make and for each of the events of good or bad luck he may encounter. So we may now rephrase our question in this somewhat more structured way. Given the complex and dramatic impact of a political settlement on citizens' individual resources, what choice of political settlement treats citizens with equal concern? What choice would the fair-minded parent of them all make, for example? What is the role of taxes in that fair-minded political settlement, and what rates of taxation would it require for people of different levels of wealth and income?

Now it might be said that government is *not* the parent of its citizens, that adult citizens must stand on their own feet, and that government should leave them free to get on with their lives as best they can without handouts through the tax system or in any other way. But that laissez-faire advice ignores the point I just made: that government simply cannot leave its citizens alone, that since anything it does affects what people have, it must take into account that consequence of whatever it does. Of course we can, if that is what a majority of us wish, create a minimalist government with few powers to do anything except maintain police forces and armies and raise only the taxes necessary to those limited powers. But that would be a political decision taken collectively by all of us in our political capacities, and we would therefore have the responsibility of showing how our decision to create a minimal state, when we might have created a government with much greater powers to help our poorer fellow citizens, treats all of us with equal concern.

Imagine this reply: "Just because everything that government does has distributive consequences, it does not follow that government should consider those consequences in deciding what to do. On the contrary, each element of the political settlement should be decided without reference to its distributive results. Let conservation policy dictate conservation laws, foreign policy dictate trade alliances, military policy dictate the military budget, and so on, and then let the distributive chips fall where they may."

This is not a possible strategy, however, because each of these policy decisions involves budget and allocation decisions, and these are automatically distributive decisions. How can officials decide how much to spend on military hardware without also deciding how much to spend on education and health care, and how can they decide those questions without a theory about what the citizens of all economic classes are entitled to have? Moreover, how can they decide how much to spend on military force without deciding how much tax it would be fair to raise, and how can they decide that without deciding from whom it would be fair to extract taxes and in what shares? There is no neutral, laissez-faire answer to that question. Even ultraconservatives would have choices to make. As I said, they would need a distributive theory even to justify choosing a minimalist government, or even to choose between the flat-rate tax scheme that some conservatives favor, which means that rich people pay at the same rate but pay more in total taxes, or Margaret Thatcher's poll tax scheme, under which everyone, rich and poor, pays exactly the same amount.

So the laissez-faire state is an illusion. Of course we can say, if we wish, that once we have fixed the political settlement in the right way, people must be left free to make such transactions with one another—about wage and price, for example—as they can, and that the state should not disturb the result of those bargains. But obviously this is not a way of avoiding the question of which political settlement treats people with equal concern; on the contrary, it assumes that the political settlement in force does just that.

We should consider one further way in which conservatives might hope to blunt the force of my question. They might claim that government treats people as equals when it pursues some collective, overall goal that does not require it to consider the fairness of the resulting distribution as an independent question. Suppose, for example, that government aims at whatever political settlement will make the community in the long run most prosperous overall, measured in aggregate financial terms, or happiest overall, measured in some psychological coin. That policy might justify very great inequality of resources—low taxes on high-income executives to encourage them to work even harder, perhaps—but it might nevertheless be said to treat everyone with equal concern because it counts the wealth or happiness of each equally in considering which policies make the community richest or happiest in aggregate.

But this appeal to aggregate goals immediately raises a further question of equal concern. The government might not have chosen an aggregate goal. Or it might have chosen a different overall goal: for example, a more complex goal that aims at aggregate prosperity or happiness but limits the inequality this might produce by providing that no one's wealth may be permitted to fall below a stipulated floor even if preventing this means that aggregate wealth or happiness is not as great as it might otherwise be. So the question must be asked: does government show equal concern for everyone if it adopts an unqualified aggregate goal as the basis for the community's political settlement rather than a different or qualified goal that would produce somewhat better lives for those at the bottom of the economic ladder? If the resulting inequality is too great, it would be hard for government to justify the claim that it has nevertheless shown equal concern through its choice of an unqualified aggregate goal. Imagine that a family is about to buy a new house and wishes to buy the house with the largest aggregate bedroom space, measured in overall square feet, that it can afford. Does it show equal concern for its members if it buys the house with the largest average bedroom size even though one bedroom, which it knows will be occupied by the youngest child, is miserably dark and insufferably small?

Personal Responsibility

My argument so far might be thought to recommend a very radical conclusion: that a government shows equal concern for all its citizens only by arranging its political settlement so that each has the same resources no matter what choices he has made and how his luck has fallen. But that is too quick a conclusion because government must also respect the second principle of human dignity, which assigns each citizen a personal responsibility to identify and realize value in his own life. There is much truth in the objection I imagined earlier to my analogy between government and a family. Adults are not children for whom someone else must or should make important decisions; indeed not even all children are children in that sense. We need a conception of equal concern that respects the personal responsibility of citizens as well as the intrinsic value of their lives, and that requirement substantially limits how far government can ensure that all citizens have the same resources available to them at all times.

Suppose, for example, a radically egalitarian economic policy that collects all the community's resources once a year and redistributes them equally so as to cancel out all the transactions of the past year and leave people free to start all over again on equal terms. That would be like sweeping up all the Monopoly money and property every quarter of an hour and beginning again, which would of course ruin the game because then no choice would have any consequences for anyone. It would not matter what anyone did. The radical egalitarian economic policy would have the same result at least financially: people would be insulated from the economic consequences of their acts and therefore unable to take any responsibility for the economic dimension of their own lives. In such a world I could not stay in school longer in order to hold a higher-paying job later or economize now in order to educate my children better or make a shrewd investment in hopes of realizing a profit. None of these choices would make any sense because I would end in the same economic position whatever I did; I could take no financial responsibility for my own choices because my own choices would have no financial consequences at all.

A less radical egalitarian program would compromise personal responsibility less thoroughly but still substantially. Consider, for example, John Rawls's much admired theory of justice, according to which a community's political settlement should aim, once important liberties are adequately protected, that the least well-off group in the community be as well-off as possible. That does not mean that all citizens should have the same money and other resources. It might well be that allowing talented people to keep more of the money they earn would encourage them to work harder, which would benefit the worst-off group because it would then have more wealth absolutely than if wealth were kept equal. Critics have objected that Rawls's principle ignores the fact that relative wealth matters as well as absolute wealth. They say that it is better when everyone has a thousand dollars than when the poorest people have two thousand and the richest millions.

I want now to make a different and in my view more serious objection, however. Rawls defines the worst-off group just in terms of the resources its members have, with no discrimination between those who are badly off because they have fallen ill or have had bad luck and those who are badly off because they have chosen not to work as hard as other people do or not to work at all. So his proposal does not make the fate of someone in this worst-off class depend in any way on that person's personal choices or responsibility; if he is in that class, he will receive whatever redistributive benefits are needed to make members of that class as rich as they can be, whichever choices he makes about work. It might improve the overall position of the worst-off class for the state to pay benefits not only to people who cannot work but to people who can work but prefer to comb beaches instead. So Rawls's scheme also cuts the connection between personal choice and personal fate that the principle of personal responsibility requires.

This is not an oversight in Rawls's theory of justice; he aimed to create what he called a political conception of justice that people could accept no matter what more comprehensive views they hold about such ethical matters as whether one should accept personal responsibility for one's situation in life. As I said in chapter 3, he hoped that in public debate people would appeal to and argue about only political principles, not private ethical ideals about how people should live their lives.[14] I explained there why I disagree. In my view we cannot construct a genuine argument in America now about the role of religion in public life if we accept such a limitation, because our distinctly political convictions are now too sharply different. We must try to identify more comprehensive ethical principles about dignity and personal responsibility that we share and then try to explore which of our conflicting political principles are more securely grounded in those more fundamental ethical convictions. We must follow the same strategy if we hope to create a public debate about the subject of this chapter. Our distinctly political views about government's responsibility for helping the poor and unfortunate among us are now starkly confrontational: the intuitions of conservatives tend to reject or limit any such public responsibility, and those of liberals tend to accept and expand it. If we hope to argue constructively with one another, we must broaden the ground of argument, and we cannot do that without including, as part of the argument, questions about the personal responsibility of people for their own economic fate. We must reject any egalitarian scheme that purports not to recognize that responsibility at all.

So the political settlement of a nation that is committed to the two principles of human dignity that I am assuming we share must satisfy two conditions that are very demanding, and it must satisfy them taken together. The nation's political settlement creates the distribution of wealth that flows from each imaginable set of personal variables—from each set of choices its citizens might make and all the good and bad luck they might encounter. That settlement must treat all those over whom the community claims dominion with equal concern, and it must also respect their personal responsibility. A theory of just taxation must therefore include not only a theory of what equal concern demands on the best understanding but also a conception of the true consequences of personal responsibility, and it must find a way to satisfy both of these requirements in the same structure.

If we are to argue sensibly about either the justice or the legitimacy of Bush's tax policies, each side, conservative and liberal, must try to construct a theory of just taxation that meets these two conditions and supports its position. In the next several sections of this chapter, I shall construct and argue for a theory that I believe clarifies the liberal position and shows its true strength. I shall then consider what plausible objections conservatives might make to my argument and attempt to reply to those objections. It remains for conservatives to construct an alternative theory for assessing tax policies in the light of their different understanding of the two principles. If they can construct a sufficiently plausible theory that justifies our present low-tax policies, then even if that theory is not wholly convincing, it would nevertheless rebut my suspicion that our present tax policy fails not only in justice but in legitimacy as well. If they cannot, that suspicion would be strengthened.

I should respond to one possible objection to this way of proceeding. It might be said that I am wrongly isolating the tax issue from other issues of social justice. It might seem that many very different kinds of political settlements in which taxes play very different roles would satisfy the two principles of human dignity and that some of these would not rely on a redistributive tax scheme very much, if at all, so that we cannot say that any particular kind of tax scheme is inevitably required for either justice or legitimacy.[15] A socialist society, for example, might assign jobs, fix wages, and provide housing, health care, and other benefits in such a way that everyone has a roughly equal standard of living; in that way it might hope to meet the requirements of equal concern without relying on the taxation and redistribution of wealth as an important weapon.

But a socialist society whose economy was so heavily controlled by collective decisions could not satisfy the further requirement that it respect personal responsibility. A community can respect that requirement only if it leaves its citizens very largely free to make their own decisions about work, leisure, investment, and consumption, and only if it leaves fixing prices and wages very largely to market forces. (I have defended that claim at length elsewhere.)[16] But if a community does allow personal choice that decisive role in fixing prices, wages, and other economic facts, and if allowing personal choice that role results in a distribution of wealth so unequal that a government of equal concern must redistribute that wealth in some way, then it must indeed rely on a tax scheme to accomplish this. So our question can properly be put as a question about what kind of tax scheme is needed in a society that both shows equal concern and respects personal freedom.

Equality Ex Post and Ex Ante

I cannot now propose a very detailed tax scheme. Too much depends on facts I do not know and that would in any case soon change. That is why I promised a tax theory rather than a detailed tax scheme. Even so, we can improve on the flabby rhetoric in which the confrontation over taxes is now expressed. Since I am concerned with the question of legitimacy as well as of justice, I shall try to construct a structure that allows us to ask not only what level and kind of taxation would be optimal but also what level would seem too low to defend as even a good-faith attempt to treat the poor with equal concern. I shall concentrate on the question of who must pay what in taxes, rather than on the equally important question of how the money raised should be spent. I shall assume only that it is to be spent in ways that reduce effective inequality within the community either through transfers of money or commodities to individuals, as through unemployment compensation or a food stamp program, or through more collective in-kind welfare programs such as public housing or state health care provision. These questions of expenditure are of course complex and important, but we focus now on the tax side of the tax-and-spend equation.

I repeat what I just emphasized. The principle of personal responsibility requires a mainly free-market economic organization so that people one by one, rather than their governments, fix the main structural elements of the economic culture in which they live, including the prices of the different kinds of goods they choose to buy and the rent of the labor they choose to offer. Only in that way can people exercise their responsibility to identify and realize value in their own lives, because only then does the price of what one person buys or produces reflect the value it has for others. Only a wide-ranging economic market respects that imperative of personal responsibility.

But of course a market produces very great inequality not just because some people make more expensive choices about how much or how little to work and what to consume, but, even more dramatically, because some people are better than others at producing what others value and some people have better luck in their investments and in their accidents and health. A community that has equal concern for all its citizens cannot simply ignore the latter variables of talent and luck because it could have chosen an entirely different political settlement that would have achieved a very different distribution with much less inequality. Even if its programs are very popular with the electorate as a whole, including those who do not benefit materially from those programs, it must be able to explain to those who are not satisfied why its choice of a market system with the structure it chose treats them with equal concern in spite of the poor position to which that choice has condemned them. Redistribution through policies of tax and spend seems the obvious solution, because taxation takes hold after people have made their choices, and it therefore affects prices and choices less than a more forced economy would do.

We must therefore begin to construct a tax theory by assuming that a community treats citizens with equal concern when its economic system allows them genuinely equal opportunities to design a life according to their own values. They have equal opportunities, let us say, when their wealth and other resources depend on the value and costs of their choices, but not on their luck, including their genetic luck in parents and talents. This ideal cannot be realized perfectly, for various reasons I have described elsewhere,[17] but we can adopt it as an ideal standard in trying to define both an optimally just tax program and a minimally redistributive tax program that is consistent with legitimacy. We now need to make a crucial distinction, however, because government might aim to make people equal in that way at different points in their lives, and it matters very much which point it selects. A technical distinction drawn from economics will be useful in explaining this choice: the distinction between *ex post* and *ex ante* equality.

A community has established full ex post equality when the differences in its citizens' wealth can be fully explained at all times by the choices they have made about whether and how much to work and how much to save or spend, when what they have depends only on those choices and has not been affected by any differences in their talents or in the luck they have had in their investments or health. So when someone's wealth falls below what other people have because he lacks the talent to work at a high-paying job that they can manage, or because he has fallen ill and is unable to work, or because he has had huge medical expenses through no fault of his own, then a government committed to ex post equality undertakes, so far as this is possible, to restore him to the position he would have held but for these disabilities or accidents. A government aims at ex ante equality, on the other hand, when it does all it can to put people in an equal position in advance of any turns of fate that might make them unequal—in advance, that is, of the events or circumstances that count as good or bad luck. It can improve ex ante equality, for example, by arranging that all citizens have an opportunity to buy on equal terms the appropriate insurance against low productive talent or bad luck.

Ex post equality might seem initially to be exactly what genuine equal concern requires. After all, someone who is badly injured or crippled and receives only an insurance settlement by way of compensation is still much worse off than if he had not been injured at all. If the community can do better by him, an equal concern for his fate would seem to argue that it should do better. Many egalitarians insist that only ex post equality will suffice as a general political ideal.

I disagree; conservatives are right to reject ex post equality as a sensible or even defensible goal. It suffers from a variety of defects that make ex ante equality a superior ideal for politics. First, a good part of the difference that luck makes in people's lives is due to investment luck. You and I both study the stock market with equal care and make equally intelligent, though different, choices. Your stocks thrive and mine wither; you are rich and I am poor, and this is only because your luck has been better than mine. But the community cannot undertake to restore me to equality with you without destroying the whole institution of economic investment and the economy along with it. If neither of us in the end gains or loses by our investment choices, our choices have been pointless, and we will cease making them. That would not only make all our lives worse but would violate our personal responsibility as well in the way I described earlier in this chapter in rejecting radical egalitarian theories of justice. Most of the important decisions we make in life are investment decisions whose outcome depends to a considerable degree on our luck. The success of any decision to train for or take up one career rather than another, for instance, normally turns on a variety of contingencies: whether we find we have the necessary talent, for example, or whether technological change makes our training useless. If the community aimed to ensure that our fate in no way depended on how these investment gambles fared—if it guaranteed that we would make the same income whether or not our choice of career turned out to be suited to our tastes or talents—it would end by seriously diminishing our own responsibility for our choices. So any plausible goal of ex post equality would have to draw a distinction between investment and other forms of luck and rule out the former as a ground for redistribution.

Second, ex post equality would be irrational as a general political ideal even if it were restricted to noninvestment luck. Any community that undertook to spend all it could to improve the position of those who had become crippled in an accident, for instance, would have nothing left to spend on anything else, and the lives of all other citizens would be miserable in consequence, because no matter how much the community spent on equipment and personal assistance, the crippled would still be worse off than they were before and the community would be bound to spend even more on them.[18] That would not reflect anyone's actual priorities, including the priorities of those who had suffered terrible injury. If the choice had been up to them, they would not have spent everything they had to buy the best possible accident insurance policy before they were injured, because they would not have thought, given the odds, that it made sense to compromise their lives in every other respect to secure the most expensive insurance. That is why ex post equality is irrational.

Some radical egalitarians might think that these are bad arguments against ex post equality because, they might say, they show only that that goal should not be carried to an extreme, that we should insist only on a reasonable degree of ex post equality, a degree that a community could afford without much damaging the institution of investment or without spending too much of the community's treasure on compensating accident victims. That relaxed formulation of the goal would be politically disastrous for liberals, however, because it would guarantee that the battle over taxes remains confrontational and impressionistic rather than structured. It offers no guidance as to what a reasonable level of ex post equality would be, and so it allows people who demand still lower taxes to declare that the costs of even the meager compensatory programs now in place are excessive because the economic damage they inflict is too great. "Reasonable" ex post equality is an undisciplined standard that leaves great room for hypocrisy and self-deceit and so offers very little protection for the poor, even in a society that embraces it enthusiastically.

In any case, we are trying to establish not only the optimal tax program for a fully just state but the minimally generous program consistent with political legitimacy, and if ex ante equality, which is less generous than full ex post equality, is defensible as an interpretation of equal concern, then we should take ex ante equality to state the minimum goal. But we need some fuller account of what ex ante equality means. It plainly involves social effort on a large front. If some workers face much higher risks of serious accident than others, then ex ante equality would be improved by programs of shop-floor safety that make those risks less unequal, for example. But I shall concentrate on the source of inequality most easily attacked through the tax system: inequality in people's ability to protect themselves against risk in advance through one or another form of insurance.

Images of Justice

Large-scale political philosophy almost always relies on metaphor and image because a theory of social justice must be animated by some vivid conception of the attitudes people should bring to their collective political and social life. Two great images have dominated theories of economic justice: the metaphor of an imaginary social contract that provides for redistribution from rich to poor and the metaphor of an insurance pool to which all members of the society contribute and from which the needy draw. The social contract image has played a greater role in political philosophy. In the seventeenth century, Thomas Hobbes imagined a social contract to describe a community of strikingly self-concerned individuals who, like business corporations, enter into contracts with one another in order to protect and aggrandize their own self-interest in the longer run. John Rawls used the contract device to a very different effect. He imagined people contracting behind what he called a veil of ignorance so that they do not know where their own distinct self-interest lies; that way of structuring the device expresses, as he explained, a postulated desire to construct fair terms for cooperation among them based on mutual respect. Rawls's contract fixes an ex post distribution of wealth: the parties agree that the worst-off group in the community will in the end be as well off as possible.

The insurance metaphor has been much less used by political philosophers than the contract metaphor, but it has played a much greater role in practical politics. The politicians of the Fabian movement in Britain, Franklin Roosevelt's New Deal in America, and the social democratic parties of postwar Europe all proposed that the redistributive programs they sponsored, like social security, workmen's compensation, and poverty relief programs, be understood as vast insurance schemes against accident, sickness, unemployment, and other forms of bad luck. The taxes people pay to finance these programs should be understood, they said, as insurance premiums and the benefits that people receive when they are ill, unemployed, or needy in some other way as insurance benefits. In that way the politicians hoped to claim the virtues of ex ante equality for these programs, because while the contract image attempts to defend ex post equality, the insurance image is committed to equality ex ante.

The contract metaphor is inspired by the old but failed dream of finding some basis for social justice in the hypothetical or assumed consent of all subjects to the reigning political order. The insurance metaphor is more realistic because taxes can indeed be seen as insurance-premium payments and also more instructive because, as we shall see, the level and structure of taxation can be guided by actual insurance markets. It is politically more powerful than the contract metaphor because it resonates in a variety of attractive ways. Describing a redistributive social program as insurance suggests social solidarity; it suggests that the citizens of a political community have reaffirmed their collective identity by pooling the risks they face. It lends the programs an aura of individual prudence and responsibility, because responsible people buy insurance to protect themselves and their families against unforeseen danger. It paints redistributive political programs not as charities bestowing their benefits as acts of grace but rather as matters of entitlement; people are entitled to collect on insurance policies because they have paid for such protection in advance. It reassures the community that its redistributive programs show fiscal discipline; respectable insurance companies are financially sound because the premium and benefit structures of a well-designed insurance program are in equilibrium. Finally it promises economic rationality for the community as a whole; an insurance scheme in which people are free to choose different levels of insurance allows them intelligently to decide how much of their wealth they should devote to risk management and how much to the rest of their lives.

So it is natural that politicians should find the insurance metaphor an attractive packaging for their programs, and the attraction of the metaphor in turn confirms the appeal of ex ante equality as a political goal. We must now consider, however, whether the metaphor is fraudulent when used in that way. For though the various virtues of efficient insurance schemes that I just described are all indeed realized under certain very artificial circumstances, these are very different from the circumstances in which those social programs operate. Suppose people of roughly equal wealth and vulnerability form a community in which each voluntarily insures along with others in a free and efficient insurance market offering equal insurance to all at the same premium rates. Then a fair and financially efficient version of ex ante equality is indeed created by the individual decisions of people, each in the exercise of his own responsibility for his own life. But if we are to treat the familiar social programs as insurance schemes, we must accept that they deviate from that ideal description in several ways.

First, the redistributive programs are typically not voluntary but mandatory. They are financed either by laws requiring people to insure to a particular level, as when employers are required to provide various forms of insurance for their workers, which means lower wages, or by tax levies that everyone must pay. Second, the citizens of actual political communities are not all of equal wealth and vulnerability: some are poorer than others, and some are more likely than others to suffer the misfortunes that the mandatory insurance schemes cover. Indeed some have already suffered some such misfortune: they have been born crippled in some way or without skills that are prized in the market. In actual insurance markets, people who are more vulnerable to risk pay higher premiums than those less vulnerable. People who have already suffered catastrophes cannot insure against them retrospectively, and insurers do not offer insurance to the poor at lower rates. Under typical redistributive programs, however, those who are more vulnerable to risks do not pay more than those who are less vulnerable, people are covered for misfortunes that befell them before the programs were instituted, and the rich pay whatever taxes finance the programs at higher rates than the poor.

So we must ask whether it is misleading to label these programs insurance schemes or to claim for them the virtues of fairness and efficiency that we associate with ordinary insurance markets. I believe and will now argue that this is not misleading. On the contrary, pursuing the insurance analogy in a systematic and detailed way is the key to constructing a compelling structure for redistributive taxation because the analogy reveals and exploits the most important reason why redistributive taxation is essential to treating citizens with equal concern. The popular intuition that connects insurance to equality is an important insight.

Hypothetical Insurance

I can quickly explain why. As I just said, if well-informed people were equal in their ability to insure against medical and economic disadvantage, and free to make such insurance decisions as they wished in an efficient insurance market, then ex ante equality would be secured even though, as life unfolded for them, these misfortunes fell more heavily on some than others. We therefore fail to achieve a decent level of ex ante equality through ordinary markets for the cardinal reason that people are *not* equal in their ability to insure. To repeat: there are three main reasons why some people are in a much worse position to secure insurance than others are. First, some people have less money and can therefore afford less insurance. Second, some people are more likely to suffer from specific misfortunes for reasons that insurance companies can discover. People with uncontrolled high blood pressure are more likely to have heart attacks, for instance, and insurers will either charge them more or refuse them insurance altogether. Third (this might be seen as an aspect of the second), the events against which some people might have wanted to insure have already occurred; they are born lacking talents that command high rent in the labor market, for example. These disabilities interact so that people who suffer from one are more likely to suffer from the others as well. We can correct for these ex ante inequalities, however, without the consequences that would make any program of ex post equality illiberal, irrational, and wholly impracticable.

We can correct for them by asking what level of insurance of different kinds we can safely assume that most reasonable people would have bought if the wealth of the community had been equally divided among them and if, though everyone knew the overall odds of different forms of bad luck, no one had any reason to think that he himself had already had that bad luck or had better or worse odds of suffering it than anyone else. That is the question I think decisive for fixing the optimal rates of redistributive tax in any political community. If, knowing what we know about people's tastes and fears and about what technology is available for treating diseases or alleviating incapacities and at what cost, we are confident that in those hypothetical circumstances almost everyone would, after reflection, purchase at least a given level of insurance against accident, disease, unemployment, or low wage—if we are confident that in most people's eyes it would be irrational *not* to purchase such insurance at that level—then we can safely assume that the reason the poor and unlucky in our community did not insure themselves to that level is that ex ante equality is impaired in the ways I just described.[19]

We can design a tax system to correct that unacceptable source of inequality by imagining what the total premium cost would be if everyone in the community bought that level of insurance and then by fixing aggregate annual taxes to provide a sum equal to that aggregate hypothetical insurance premium. By hypothesis, the aggregate premium would produce enough revenue that the community could then provide compensation to those with bad luck in the amount they would have been entitled to have if everyone had bought insurance at that level. That compensation might take the shape of direct transfers—for medical cost reimbursements or unemployment compensation, for instance—or public spending to provide the benefits such people would have insured to have through a single-payer health care system, for example.

That is the general structure I propose for reflecting on and debating fair levels of taxation for our political community.[20] We can carry the structure into considerable detail by speculating further about the likely insurance market in the hypothetical circumstances of fairness that I imagine: when people have roughly equal wealth and are equally vulnerable to the risks against which they would like to insure. It seems plain, to take one example, that in such a market the premiums people pay would depend on their future income; those who earned more would pay more for the same insurance coverage. Economists use another term, "expected well-being," that is useful in explaining why. Your expected well-being is calculated by imagining how well or badly off you would be if your life took different courses and then determining your average welfare in these different possible lives, taking into account the likelihood of each. People buy insurance with an eye to their expected well-being; they want to be not too badly off if bad things happen but also not too much worse off if bad things do not happen than they would have been if they had not paid insurance premiums.

We are imagining people buying insurance to protect their well-being if they turn out to have little productive talent, to have bad employment luck, or to suffer serious and expensive illnesses or accidents. Such insurance would be expensive, and buyers would try to keep the real cost of the premiums—the impact of paying the premiums on their expected well-being—as low as possible. Because an extra dollar is much more important to poor people than to rich ones—economists say that money has "declining marginal utility"—people would do this most efficiently by basing their premiums on their actual income so that the percentage of their income they paid in premiums would rise as their income rises, and those who turn out to have lower income would pay substantially less than they would if everyone paid at the same rate. If we modeled our tax structure on the hypothetical insurance story, therefore, we would insist on a fairly steep progressive-tax-rate system so that those with more income would pay at a higher rate. Flat-rate tax schemes would be offensive to our ideal of ex ante equality.

Should the main revenue-producing taxes continue to be income taxes? Or should they be consumption taxes that encourage savings, as several economists have recommended? If we did increase the share of revenue raised by consumption taxes, great care would be needed both to keep the aggregate level of taxation as high and the rates as progressive as the hypothetical insurance story requires. A regressive national sales tax, requiring everyone to pay the same tax on purchases, would obviously be illegitimate. There is also the question of estate or inheritance taxes, which are a prominent feature of tax schemes around the world but which Republicans have opposed for a generation by calling them taxes on dying. Nothing is more symbolic of conservative faith in an economic class system than their ambition to eliminate estate taxes altogether.

But some of the conservative objections to the estate tax have merit. It does seem unprincipled to tax an estate at the same rate without regard to the number or wealth of its beneficiaries. It is, moreover, hard to justify a tax on estates on the hypothetical insurance model of ex ante fairness. It would be much fairer, and more consistent with ex ante equality, to treat substantial gifts of any form, including bequests, as income subject to ordinary taxes.[21] If rates were properly progressive, however, this category of one-time, nonrepeatable income should be subject to special rules, allowing the recipient to amortize the income over several years.

Legitimacy and Counterarguments

I have discussed elsewhere several other important issues about the hypothetical insurance approach and its implications for the details of a working tax structure.[22] I shall not continue to discuss those details here, but want instead to emphasize my main conclusion: taxes are fair only when they provide at least the minimum we can safely assume that reflective people would have insured to provide for themselves if they were ex ante equal in the way I described. Economists would no doubt disagree as to the best answer to that rather complex counterfactual question; they would disagree about how much of what kinds of insurance it is safe to assume people would have bought in the imagined situation, and therefore about what level of taxation is needed to provide ex ante equality retrospectively. But no one could think that America's present tax policies are justified on that test. A great many Americans cannot afford even minimal medical care when they are seriously ill; many Americans who are unemployed cannot afford even the most frugal housing or nutrition for themselves and their families. No one could seriously propose that these Americans would not have bought enough insurance for themselves if they had had the same opportunity to buy insurance as their more prosperous or fortunate fellow citizens have, so that they could have had better lives than that.

Earlier in this chapter I distinguished the question of justice from the different question of legitimacy. I asked whether the level of indifference the nation now shows to the fate of its poor calls into question not only the justice of its fiscal policies but also their legitimacy. That depends on whether the government's policies can be understood as showing equal concern to the poor on at least some plausible account of what equal concern requires. I have now argued that equal concern requires that government aim to achieve ex ante equality among its citizens, that the hypothetical insurance test provides the best account of what ex ante equality requires, and that our present financial policies cannot conceivably be thought to provide that form of equality on that test. So it is urgent that we now ask how those who would defend the government's economic policies might reply to my argument and whether they can offer any other structure for fixing fair taxes that reflects a different but nevertheless plausible conception of equal concern for all.

Prosperity. The Bush administration claims that low taxes are good for the economy as a whole. As I said, this is a dubious claim that is rejected by many prominent economists. Taxes are significantly lower for the rich than they were in the Clinton administration, and the economic position of most people is worse. The main assumption on which the claim is based—that rich people work harder and are more productive when their taxes are low—is counterintuitive and remains undemonstrated.[23] But let us suppose, for the sake of the argument, that overall prosperity is indeed improved, all else being equal, when taxes are lower. By itself that shows nothing now pertinent because it does not speak to fairness. A nation that improves overall prosperity by lowering taxes may be like the family I imagined improving the average size of bedrooms by buying a house in which some of the bedrooms are only miserable cupboards. Legitimacy is a matter of equal concern for people, not concern for some abstract statistic.

It has been suggested that in the long run everyone benefits from increased general prosperity because this creates jobs and allows wealth at the top to "trickle down" to everyone. But that claim seems false because even in periods of considerable national prosperity, as in the Clinton administration, the position of the poor did not improve much. It is not even clear that what we call the middle class has benefited from Bush's tax cuts, and certainly the poor have not benefited. The only clear winners are those who were already rich. It may be that people have a very long run in mind; they mean that we should be thinking not of benefits to be achieved in a few years but over generations. But the longer the run, the less relevant is the hypothesis because, as John Maynard Keynes pointed out, in the very long run we will all be dead. We owe our equal concern to those now alive, not only or even primarily to their and our speculative descendants, whose very identity will anyway depend on how fair to the poor we are now.

Safety Net. So we must try to construct a conservative response that speaks to fairness, not prosperity. Conservatives might object to my argument at a very basic level. They might say that equal concern does not demand even ex ante equality, that it is good enough if the community provides a kind of safety net, a decent life for everyone, without guaranteeing anyone any form or measure of actual equality. It is perhaps a sufficient reply that our present political settlement does not even provide a safety net. It does not prevent many Americans from crashing to what any of us would consider an unacceptable and quite unsafe misery. But the objection is so basic that we should consider its premise: if government satisfies its citizens' most basic needs, it need not aim at any form of economic equality among them.

In fact, many distinguished philosophers, including liberal philosophers, have questioned whether equality is a proper political goal. We should aim, they say, at a minimal decent standard of life for everyone without taking up the further goal of guaranteeing that everyone's standard of life be the same. But as that formulation reveals, these philosophers assume that equality means ex post equality. I agree with them and with any conservative who adopts their argument that ex post equality is a dramatically unrealistic and, I would add, unfair goal. The important contrast is between ex ante equality, enforced through something like the insurance device, and some other standard of the minimum we owe everyone out of equal concern. But we cannot draw that contrast or choose between these alternatives without some argument why a lower safety net than the hypothetical insurance story justifies is acceptable, and none has been provided. The insurance device *is* a safety-net device: it sets a floor. But it is a principled safety net: we can defend it as a legitimate interpretation of what equal concern demands. What argument could fix and justify a lower degree of protection?

The Insurance Device. Conservatives might pitch their objection at a less basic level. They might accept ex ante equality as an ideal but disagree that the hypothetical insurance device is well constructed to serve that ideal. Such arguments might be available, and I would welcome them as contributing to a genuine argument about fair taxation. But I do not know what form they would take and so cannot anticipate them. Or conservatives might accept the hypothetical insurance test but argue that in fact people in the hypothetical situation would buy much less insurance than I assume they would or would reject the progressive premium rate structure I said they would embrace. Once again, I would welcome such arguments but cannot anticipate them.

We Can't Afford It. Conservatives are more likely to make rather different arguments, however. They might concede that hypothetical insurance would indeed be a fair method of designing taxes but insist that we cannot afford to be fair in that way because spending that much on the poor would bankrupt the community. Or that taking as much from the rich as the insurance argument would justify would mean leveling down to equal misery. These objections are misplaced, however; they show a misunderstanding of ex ante equality and of the insurance device. Ex post equality, if it were ever politically possible to pursue it, would indeed bankrupt the community and would impose equal misery. But the hypothetical insurance device is constructed so as to guarantee that we can afford the kind of equality it justifies.

It asks what portion of their assumed equal wealth people would devote to insurance against future tragedy or disappointment, and no rational person would commit so much to insurance that he could not live a comfortable life if these contingencies did not materialize. That holds for those who turn out rich as well as poor; I have assumed that people would make premiums sensitive to wealth, but they would not agree to premiums so high that they would be reduced to misery by those payments even if they had had economic success. It is said that a high tax policy is unaffordable because the globalization of the economy means that capital would then flee to countries with lower taxes, jeopardizing American jobs. Perhaps that is an argument for levying taxes in a way that makes capital flight more difficult or unlikely—for example, since America taxes citizens on their worldwide income, emphasizing personal income or consumption taxes rather than taxes on business might reduce incentives to locate business abroad.[24] In any case, the hypothetical insurance exercise takes all such factors into account, because our calculation of the premiums that would be required for any given level of unemployment compensation insurance, for instance, would reflect our assumptions about the impact on economic activity if everyone insured at that level. I am not now arguing, remember, that we should tax ourselves up to the highest level at which we might find it plausible to suppose that people would buy insurance at that level in the hypothetical circumstances. Even then, the objection would be misplaced because, again by hypothesis, we could afford that much in taxation. But I am now arguing only that we must tax ourselves at least to the level below which it would be wholly implausible to suppose people would not insure. The objection that we cannot afford fairness is even sillier against that more modest claim.

Liberty. If taxes continue to be cut, particularly if war and other expenses continue to balloon, the federal government will have less money to spend on a variety of other programs: conservation, safety in the workplace, income support, and Medicare and Medicaid, for example. For liberals, that is a strong argument against tax reductions, but for conservatives it is a strong argument for them. They believe that such programs threaten individual liberty and that low taxes are therefore a good strategy for protecting liberty. Some conservatives express that strategy in a slogan: we must starve the beast, they say—the beast is the federal government—to free ourselves from its tyranny. This suggestion misunderstands the character of liberty as a political value. As I said in chapter 3, no defensible conception of liberty makes government programs like unemployment relief, food stamps, and Medicaid violations of the liberty of the subjects.

The contrary conclusion of some conservatives is rooted in an enthusiasm for states' rights against the power of the national government. This is not the place to consider whether and how the burden of redistributive taxation should be divided between states and the national government in the United States. I am concerned only with what legitimacy requires of the overall structure of our government. But I can hazard the guess that most of those who want to starve the beast at the federal level would not be enthusiastic about expensive welfare and other redistributive programs more locally. They want to starve all the beasts, great and little, that might take money from them. There may be more to this objection than I see, but it will have to be pointed out to me.

Prior Ownership: It's Your Money. This is emotionally the most potent of the arguments that conservatives make for low taxes, but it is also the most confused.[25] The argument begins in the assumption that people are morally entitled to dispose as they think best of what they have earned in investments and salary or what they have inherited. It is their money, and government has no right to take it from them and give it to others. This claim challenges my argument at the deepest possible level because people who accept it can concede that government owes all its citizens equal concern and even that it should therefore work toward reducing ex ante inequality in the nation, and yet insist that government must do that with its own proper resources and not play Robin Hood by stealing from its prosperous citizens and giving their money to the poor. They can even concede that wealthy citizens have a moral obligation of charity: they should voluntarily share what they have with those less fortunate. But it does not follow that government may force them to do what they should; that is a form of tyranny. Anyway, conservatives say, you know better what to do with your money than Washington does, and Washington must respect your decisions.

Even people who embrace this argument accept that government has some responsibilities. It must protect its citizens from crime and foreign enemies, including terrorists, and that is very expensive indeed. So government must raise money to provide the security and other benefits and protections that economists call public goods: goods that benefit everyone, rich and poor alike. But—the conservatives I have in mind say—that does not justify raising funds for the very different purpose of welfare entitlements; these do not benefit everyone alike, and it is wrong to make everyone pay for them. Nor does the public-goods rationale justify making the rich pay more than an equal share for what everyone receives. There might be some case for a flat-rate tax in which everyone pays at the same rate of his income or wealth— and the rich therefore pay more in total—rather than for a poll tax of the kind Prime Minister Thatcher of Britain favored, in which each citizen pays exactly the same amount in taxes for services available to all. A flat-rate tax respects the principle that since the rich have more property to protect from domestic and foreign enemies, they should contribute a higher amount per person by paying at the same rate. But there is no excuse whatsoever for compounding the inequality by asking them to pay for that protection at higher tax rates as well.

This is the heart of the moral case for a flat-rate tax. Since it is your money that the government takes, and since it takes your money without your consent, you should at least pay only for what you get. We must now ask, however, what the ground is supposed to be of my moral entitlement to keeping the money I have been paid in salary or dividends or inherited from my parents. You may say, I am entitled to it because it was my effort and talent that produced it or because people whose money it was decided to give it to me. But what I or they earn from any given expenditure of effort and talent or from any investment luck depends entirely on the political settlement in force when we earned it, so it wholly begs the question to say that I am entitled to a particular political settlement—to one that reduces my taxes, for instance—because it better protects what I have earned or been given. If we changed the political settlement in some important way, I would earn or inherit less or more. We must also reject, for the same reason, the parallel argument that because my contribution to the economy's success is reflected in my annual salary, I am entitled to keep that salary as my reward for that contribution. My salary measures my contribution only against the background of a particular political settlement; my supposed contribution measured in that way would be less or more if that background settlement were different. So once again it begs the question to suppose that I have "earned" my present salary in order to justify the claim that government should let me keep that salary. If any component of the political settlement, including the tax component, were different, I would have earned a different salary.

So the usual arguments that supposedly demonstrate that pretax income is "my" money are incoherent. The only coherent such argument supposes that the accident of first possession gives rise to a moral entitlement. Our federal income tax system, which is the tax system most Americans have in mind when they argue that taxes should be lower, delays the incidence of taxation in a variety of ways. Most people pay taxes that are taken out of their pay packet before they receive their wages, but these taxes appear as a deduction from a larger sum designated as income on their pay slips. Rich people are permitted to delay paying some of their taxes; they pay them in quarterly installments of estimated tax topped up by a final payment on April 15. In that way they pay out money that has previously been registered as in their possession in a bank account or investment adviser's report. But these are mere accidents of efficient tax accounting. Taxes can be and are paid in other ways that do not include any earlier registration of wealth possession. Everyone could pay through deductions at source, or through payroll taxes that are paid by employers, and have the effect of lowering the salaries an employer pays without listing any larger sum as the employee's initial salary. There is no magic in mere first possession, and the fact that a rich person briefly holds the money that he will later pay in taxes in no way argues that he owns that money morally.

The Challenge

The gap between America's rich and poor seems indefensible. The poor have no adequate health provision; a great many of them have no health provision at all. They lack adequate housing, and their nutrition is terrible. Their children are born with exceptionally bleak prospects for the rest of their lives. It is not possible to think that sensible people would have run the risk of that misery if they did not have to. If my overall argument is right, it follows that the very legitimacy of our political society is now threatened.

That threat can be dissolved only if those who defend conservative tax policies can construct a rival case that shows how these policies can after all be seen as demonstrating equal concern for the poor. I tried to anticipate arguments they might make. But it is their turn now. What case can they make to rescue the legitimacy of what we as a nation have done to our poor? Does political legitimacy not require equal concern? Is ex ante rather than ex post equality the appropriate measure of what equal concern demands? If not, what is the appropriate measure? If so, is the hypothetical insurance strategy not at the heart of any successful account of ex ante equality? Does that strategy not require a substantial increase in the taxes paid for redistributive programs by the richest sections of our community? The conservative culture must take up those questions if we are to regain genuine argument for our politics. Who on that side will begin?

CHAPTER 5

IS DEMOCRACY POSSIBLE?

Is America Democratic?

I HAVE PRESSED TWO main claims in this book. I said, first, that though we appear to be fiercely divided between two political cultures about human rights, religion, and taxes, among many other issues, we have not managed to construct even the beginnings of a decent public argument about these matters. Second, I suggested that we can construct an argument from common ground if we begin way back, at a distinctly philosophical level, in twin principles of human dignity that we almost all accept. But do we have the kind of political system that might accommodate a genuine debate?

No nation's politics can be run like a philosophy seminar; a democracy must give the final verdict on who leads it to many millions of people who have no training in economics, philosophy, foreign policy, or environmental science and who do not have the time or perhaps the ability to achieve much competence in these disciplines. But our national politics fails the standards of even a decent junior high school debate. Our candidates make us squirm with embarrassment when they clear their throats to speak. They are ruled by consultants who tell them that style is everything and content nothing, that they must say as little as possible except in subliminal codes meant secretly to energize important groups, that a punchy sound bite on the evening news is political gold, that anything remotely resembling an actual argument is death.

So Americans are horribly misinformed and ignorant about the most important issues. Bruce Ackerman and James Fishkin, in their interesting book *Deliberation Day*, make our hair stand on end.[1] Polls show that just before the 2004 election, half of all Americans thought that Iraqis were among the 9/11 hijackers. At the height of the cold war, a majority of Americans did not know whether Russia was a member of NATO. In 1996 pollsters set out a long list of questions about current events that they deemed critical to the election that year; no more than half the public polled could answer even 40 percent of those questions. Given that level of ignorance, it is inevitable that politicians compete with one another on soap-opera standards. Who looks more confident or calmer? Who talks your language? Which one would you rather date?

The vicious spiral winds down and down. If the political consultants tell the politicians to treat us as ignorant, we will remain ignorant, and so long as we are ignorant, the consultants will tell the politicians to treat us that way. No candidate can afford to jump off that spiral; they all worry that the public is so accustomed to down-market politics that it will punish anyone who disturbs it with a syllogism. Truth as a gold standard has become obsolete: politicians never seek accuracy in describing their own records or their opponents' positions. They seek the maximal distortion that leaves some tiny fig leaf of truth intact somewhere in the fine print.

We know that money is the curse of our politics. Candidates and political parties collect enormous sums to finance their various electoral campaigns, and this practice corrupts politics and government for several well-rehearsed reasons. Politicians spend grotesquely more effort in raising money than they do on reflecting on policy or principle. Parties made rich by the contributions of great financial interests have an enormous advantage in the competition for votes, and new and poor political organizations are for that reason alone at a usually fatal disadvantage. Large campaign contributors purchase what is euphemistically called "access" to officials; in fact they often purchase not merely access but control. Big money poisons politics in yet another way, moreover, which is less often noticed. It puts enormous sums at the disposal of politicians and their consultants, which makes possible the hugely expensive television and radio campaigns of glitz, slander, and endless repetition of half-truths and pointless factoids that have become the lifeblood of our dumbed-down politics. No candidate can risk sitting out this ugly dance: he who hesitates down-market is lost. In politics money is the enemy not just of fairness but of real argument.

Journalism is supposed to help; journalists are supposed to be indispensable to democracy, the ombudsmen of truth. That is the justification most often given for the special protection of freedom of the press in our Constitution's First Amendment. But television journalism is what matters now—until the Internet takes over, if it ever does—and television journalism is part of the problem, not the cure. Networks are owned by conglomerates with bottom lines, and news competes with the rest of the schedule for entertainment value. So television trades mainly in sound bites that politicians must compose and repeat endlessly, and its journalistic sister, radio, trades mainly in call-in talk shows aimed at some preselected political group it can tell advertisers to count on. Negative campaigning works, in spite of everyone's pious hopes that it won't, simply because negative campaigning is more fun to watch or hear. Rupert Murdoch's Fox News may not be a new phenomenon—party-line newspapers with no scruples have long been a feature of yellow journalism—but it is new in its scale: a gigantic attack dog with an ultraconservative agenda and a knockout schedule of sports and *The Simpsons* that captures huge audiences for its shamelessly biased news and current affairs programs.

How bad is all this? We might take one of two views. We might say that whether our politics is satisfactory or unsatisfactory is a matter of taste, and that those who think it very unsatisfactory are likely to be those whose candidates lost the last election. True, some people would relish a more enlightened style of political argument of the kind once found, for example, in Britain. But others think our style is better suited to our national temperament, that through what I persist in calling dumbed-down politics, Americans are uncannily able to choose leaders of quality whose values shine through the kind of politics we have developed better than they would in something more like a university debate. It was widely reported by commentators that Senator Kerry won his 2004 presidential debates with President Bush handily. But in the end Bush impressed the public more with his character than Kerry did with his arguments. Reason isn't everything, after all, and emotion, of the kind American elections specialize in, has an important place in politics.

That is one, rather sanguine, view we might take. As I said, people who are happy with the results of recent elections might well incline to that view of our politics. Here is the other, very different view: our politics are now so debased that they threaten our standing as a genuine democracy—that they have begun to undermine, that is, the legitimacy of our political order. Is that far-fetched? It is common ground among us that democracy is an indispensable form of government. Some of us may question whether it is America's mission to foster democratic governments in the rest of the world, as President Bush now says it is, but none of us questions the superiority of democracy for us to any other form of government we might have. Indeed none of us questions that, at least for us, a democratic government is the only legitimate form of government, that no other form of government would have moral title to command allegiance over us.

That broad agreement is deceptive, however, because we disagree very much among ourselves—now largely along the familiar red-blue lines—about what democracy really is. Whether we are satisfied with our democracy turns on what we think democracy really is. I shall describe two conceptions of democracy. If we accept one of these, we may think that America is the paradigm of a democratic society and is therefore well placed to lead other nations in that direction. If we accept the other, we must conclude that America falls far short of being a true democracy and that it may not be possible for us to become one. Which of these conceptions of democracy is right? How can partisans of each defend their position to partisans of the other?

What Is Democracy?

The two views of democracy that are in contest are these. According to the *majoritarian* view, democracy is government by majority will, that is, in accordance with the will of the greatest number of people, expressed in elections with universal or near universal suffrage. There is no guarantee that a majority will decide fairly; its decisions may be unfair to minorities whose interests the majority systematically ignores. If so, then the democracy is unjust but no less democratic for that reason. According to the rival *partnership* view of democracy, however, democracy means that the people govern themselves each as a full partner in a collective political enterprise so that a majority's decisions are democratic only when certain further conditions are met that protect the status and interests of each citizen as a full partner in that enterprise. On the partnership view, a community that steadily ignores the interests of some minority or other group is just for that reason not democratic even though it elects officials by impeccably majoritarian means. This is only a very sketchy account of the partnership conception, however. If we find the more familiar majoritarian conception unsatisfactory, we shall have to develop the partnership view in more detail.

The United States is certainly not a pure example of the majoritarian conception of democracy. The framers did not intend it to be because they limited the power of political majorities in various ways: they provided a set of individual constitutional rights, like the right of free speech, as trumps over the majority's power. So it is no automatic objection to the Supreme Court's decisions about abortion, for example, that a majority of citizens would reject those decisions. But we might think that the United States should be a majoritarian democracy with only such limitations, by way of individual rights, as our Constitution embodies. Then we could not count the impoverished state of our politics as itself a defeat in that democratic ambition because there is nothing in the majoritarian conception that requires the kind of argumentative political culture that we lack.

The people, after all, are not crying out for more sophisticated political argument; they are busy, they do not mind being entertained, and the great majority of them know what they think anyway. If they thought it important to have better argument, then politicians would at least try harder to supply it. Many more people could watch the public broadcasting networks or C-span if they wished or could read the *New York Times* or the news pages of the *Wall Street Journal*. If they prefer to watch Fox News, they are only exercising their democratic right to decide for themselves how to prepare for the franchise. It would be very wrong for government to try to force the public to attend to what apparently bores it. Regulation of that kind would presuppose that individual voters have a democratic responsibility to attend to and try to understand the arguments that appeal to other voters. That assumption is entirely foreign to the majoritarian conception. Perhaps some people do accept some such responsibility, but the democratic verdict is not less legitimate when most do not, because democracy is only about how political opinions are now distributed in the community, not how those opinions came to be formed. So if we adopt the majoritarian view of democracy as the right one, then what I called the sanguine view of our politics is perfectly understandable.

If we aim to be a partnership democracy, on the other hand, the degraded state of our political argument does count as a serious defect in our democracy because mutual attention and respect are the essence of partnership. We do not treat someone with whom we disagree as a partner—we treat him as an enemy or at best as an obstacle—when we make no effort either to understand the force of his contrary views or to develop our own opinions in a way that makes them responsive to his. The partnership model so described seems unattainable now because it is difficult to see how Americans on rival sides of the supposed culture wars could come to treat each other with that mutual respect and attention. That is why, if we decide that the partnership conception is the only defensible account of democracy, we must wonder whether real democracy is now possible in the United States. But partnership democracy is certainly a possible aspiration for us. We can try to move closer to it, if we wish, in ways I shall try to suggest.

Our choice between these two understandings of democracy is crucial for many reasons. The institutions of democracy are often thought to provide a response to criticisms of the kind I have been making against our present government in the last three chapters. In chapter 4, for example, I said that our legitimacy is threatened when we refuse to tax ourselves enough to save our fellow citizens from hopelessly bleak and dangerous lives. If we accept the majoritarian view of democracy, however, then there is an apparently powerful reply to my claim, which is that the American people have endorsed the tax policy that I questioned by reelecting Bush, however narrowly, and that democracy therefore legitimates the policy I condemned. Suppose Congress were suddenly converted by the force of the argument for higher taxes and adopted huge tax increases that it used to fund wonderful redistributive programs. Congress's behavior would in many ways be admirable, but, so long as it had not first persuaded the majority of people and they still wanted lower taxes, it would in at least one dimension be wrong. Justice might smile on what Congress had done, but if the majoritarian conception is correct, democracy would frown.

That is a pertinent response to my charges only if we do accept that majoritarian conception, however, because on the rival partnership view the response that the majority favors low taxes simply begs the crucial question, which is whether the majority is entitled by the right theory of democracy to treat a minority in that way. That contrast brings out the crucial difference between the two conceptions of democracy. The majoritarian conception purports to be purely procedural and therefore independent of other dimensions of political morality; it allows us to say, as I indicated, that a decision is democratic even if it is very unjust. But the partnership conception does not make democracy independent of the rest of political morality; on that conception we need a theory of equal partnership to decide what is or is not a democratic decision, and we need to consult ideas about justice, equality, and liberty in order to construct such a theory. So on the partnership conception, democracy is a substantive, not a merely procedural, ideal. I said, in chapter 3, that we cannot construct an adequate theory of liberty without relying on other political virtues in our definition. The partnership conception makes a parallel claim about democracy.

That difference might seem to count heavily in favor of the majoritarian conception because that conception allows us to identify a distinct, procedural value of political organization. It allows us to say that a particular political decision—to reduce taxes, for example—at least has the virtue of democratic legitimacy and then ask, as an independent question, whether the decision that has that virtue nevertheless suffers from defects. The majoritarian conception, that is, appears to have the advantage of separating discrete values that the partnership conception fuses together. But that is an advantage only if the bare fact that a majority prefers some policy, just on its own, *does* provide at least some reason in favor of that policy. If, on the contrary, the bare fact of majority support supplies no reason at all why a community should adopt the policy it supports, even a weak reason that might be overcome by contrary considerations, then the apparent advantage of the majoritarian conception becomes a great disadvantage because that conception would then claim to find some distinct value where there is no value to be found.

So we must choose between the two conceptions by asking whether majority support just on its own does supply some form of moral reason for what the majority supports, and I shall shortly turn to that complex question. First, however, it is worth noticing how quietly our two political cultures, red and blue, now divide in their enthusiasm for one or the other conception. The other divisions I have been discussing—about religion, taxes, and the human rights of suspected terrorists—are explicit and noisy. This division is not: there are no banners proclaiming for the majoritarian or partnership conception of democracy. That is because most people's views about the character of true democracy are governed by their sense of which kind of democracy is more likely to produce the substantive political decisions they prefer. Just now conservatives appeal more to the rhetoric of majoritarianism, and liberals more to that of partnership, but these positions were often reversed in the past and may be reversed again. Conservatives who are hostile to redrawing electoral districts so as to give more political power to historical minorities appeal to a majoritarian conception, for example. They say that any effort to give one group more power per member than it would have on a more random or color-blind districting is offensive to democracy. Liberals who support racial districting favor a partnership conception because this recommends arrangements that improve the status of historically embattled minorities as full democratic partners.

In recent decades the main battles about the nature of democracy have been fought over judges and over the Supreme Court's authority to declare acts of other branches of government unconstitutional. The American Constitution limits the power of political majorities by recognizing individual constitutional rights that majorities may not infringe. Conservatives accuse judges of inventing new rights and reading them into the Constitution as a means of substituting their own personal values for those of the majority. We noticed, in chapter 3, some of the past judicial decisions that conservatives particularly hate: the Supreme Court's school prayer, abortion, and homosexual rights decisions, for example. Conservatives say that allowing judges to make those fundamental decisions is undemocratic because it denies the majority the right and power to make fundamental moral decisions for itself. Liberals, on the contrary, have over the last half-century mainly applauded the role and decisions of the so-called activist judges because they approve the decisions that outrage conservatives. They think that the decisions that expanded individual rights enhanced rather than savaged our democracy, and that view presupposes the partnership conception. It is no objection, for liberals, that the judges who make these decisions cannot be thrown out by the people because according to the partnership conception the majority is entitled to its will only when the conditions of full partnership are met, and liberals think that the controversial constitutional decisions helped to ensure that the conditions are met.

Judges can outrage conservatives in other ways as well, as became plain in the drama about Terri Schiavo, the young woman I mentioned in chapter 3 who had been in a persistent vegetative state for fifteen years when a Florida state court judge, on the application of Mrs. Schiavo's husband, ordered the feeding tubes that kept her alive withdrawn. The conservative Congress passed emergency legislation purporting to give federal judges power to review that decision and to order the feeding tubes restored pending their decision. The federal judge who was assigned the case by lot refused to order the tubes restored or to overrule the Florida court. The Fourth Circuit Court of Appeals, a court generally regarded as very conservative, quickly upheld the federal judge's ruling, and the Supreme Court as quickly refused to intervene. Prominent Republicans then announced themselves outraged at what they took to be the insubordination of all these judges. Once Congress had made its will known, they said, it was the duty of judges to execute that will because Congress is elected by and represents the majority of the people. Tom DeLay, then the majority leader of the House, declared that the judges should be impeached for that subordination, and though other Republicans dissociated themselves from his inflammatory remarks, it became plain that they too assumed that the will of the people expressed through Congress was supreme and brooked no judicial opposition. Liberals were in turn outraged by the Republican reaction; they said that the Republicans were rejecting the independence of the judiciary and the rule of law. Disagreement about the nature of democracy shone through this confrontation. Conservatives assumed and liberals denied the greater democratic legitimacy of the legislative to the judicial branch of government, a claim presupposed by any consistent version of the majoritarian conception of democracy.

Judges are also at the center of another recent and important constitutional drama, but this time it is the method of appointing them, not their powers once they are appointed, that is in dispute. Republicans now control the Senate, but they fall short of the sixty votes they need to break a filibuster, that is, to close off debate on any issue. In his first term President Bush ignored the advice of Democratic leaders in the Senate to consult with them in advance of judicial nominations in order to avoid bruising confirmation battles. Instead, with no consultation, he nominated a raft of ultraconservative judges designed to please only his ultra-right-wing power base. The Senate Democrats successfully used filibusters to block a few of the nominees they deemed particularly unqualified. Republican leaders then threatened to amend the Senate rules to abolish the possibility of filibuster in considering judicial nominations so that the Republican majority could confirm all of Bush's rejected nominees, no matter how reactionary or unqualified. Fourteen influential senators, seven from each party, agreed to a compromise that shelved that plan, at least temporarily, in return for Democrats' agreement not to filibuster against confirming some judges Bush had nominated. But the compromise was drafted in vague terms and may collapse at any time.

The Republican leadership said that a filibuster is undemocratic because it allows a minority of forty-one senators to thwart the will of the Senate majority by refusing to bring a nomination to a final vote. Their argument appeals to the majoritarian conception of democracy. In fact their argument is weak even if we accept that conception because the Senate is a nonmajoritarian body. Each state elects two senators, no matter how big or small its population, and the Democratic senators, though fewer in number, in fact now represent more people than the larger number of Republican senators do. But plainly it is the majoritarian conception that the Republicans have in mind when they call filibusters undemocratic. The Democrats who defend the filibuster—and moderate Republicans who are nervous about destroying that technique because they know that one day they will be in the minority—appeal to the spirit of the partnership conception to justify their position. They say that the Senate exists as a chamber of reflection, that it is designed to protect minorities against hasty majoritarian legislation, and that the filibuster has served that purpose well by requiring the majority party not simply to ride roughshod over the fundamental interests the minority party believes it must protect.

As I said, people's opinions about the nature of democracy are likely to be driven by what they believe to be the best means of realizing their other political goals. Political enthusiasms for judicial activism were very different in the early twentieth century, when an economically conservative Supreme Court was declaring progressive social legislation unconstitutional. Conservatives then appealed to something at least like the partnership conception to insist that respect for private property is indispensable to true democracy, and liberals embraced a majoritarian conception to denounce the Court's interference with social progress. In recent years conservative judges and Supreme Court justices have once again become active in striking down congressional legislation in order to increase the power of states to make their own decisions about whether, for example, handguns can legally be sold near public schools. Liberals are therefore beginning to rediscover the supposed virtues of the majoritarian conception of democracy. Liberals hated the filibuster when southern Democrats used it in the mid-twentieth century to thwart civil rights legislation, and they may come to hate it again if some unforeseen change in American politics catapults them back into power again. But the choice between the two visions of democracy will remain crucial to political morality no matter how the politics of the choice shift. It is crucial because the question I posed at the beginning of this chapter—whether the embarrassing state of our political discourse damages our democratic credentials—turns on how we choose.

Is There Any Value in Majority Rule?

Nothing is more familiar than the principle of majority vote. It is very common for people to assume that if a group is cast together in some project and must make collective decisions about matters on which they disagree, then the right procedure is to vote with each member of the group having a single vote and the verdict falling on the decision that attracts the most votes. The reasons for the wide appeal of this idea are unclear, however. If the principle of majority rule is a matter of basic and innate fairness applicable across all contexts of decision, that argues very strongly for the majoritarian conception of democracy. Any other version of democratic procedures would cheat some people—those who are in the majority on some important issue—of what they are in all fairness entitled to have. If, however, the majority rule principle is fair only once certain prior conditions of association are met, then that might argue for the partnership conception, which liberals, at least now, seem to favor.

In fact, it is a serious mistake to think that a majority vote is always the appropriate method of collective decision whenever a group disagrees about what its members should do. Suppose passengers are trapped in a lifeboat on the high seas that will sink unless one person—any person—jumps or is thrown overboard. How shall the group decide who is to be sacrificed? It seems perfectly fair to draw straws or in some other way to let fate decide. That gives each person the same chance of staying alive. Letting the group vote, however, seems a very bad idea because kinship, friendships, enmities, jealousies, and other forces that should not make a difference will then be decisive. We use lotteries to make some fateful political decisions as well. When we draft soldiers, we do not hold referendums on who should be drafted. We choose by lot. Perhaps we should make more use of chance in politics. The Athenians selected their leaders by lot, and it is not vividly clear that the quality of our legislators would decline if we chose them in the same way.

In some circumstances a group disagrees not just about how its members should act but about whether a group decision on the matter at issue is necessary at all. Suppose the question arises in some group whether consensual sexual relations are immoral outside marriage. Some members might think that a collective decision on that matter is desirable so that those who flout the majority's opinion may be punished in some way. But others deny that a collective decision is appropriate; they believe people should decide for themselves. It would beg the question against the latter opinion to hold a vote to decide whether a collective decision is appropriate. If the latter opinion is right, allowing the majority to decide even that question would be unfair.

So majority rule is by no means always an appropriate decision-making procedure. Now consider a very different suggestion. Majority rule is appropriate in politics not because it is the only fair method but for the more practical reason that majority rule results in wiser and better government. There is a venerable formal version of that argument, developed by the great mathematician Condorcet. He demonstrated that if we assume that each member of a group, on his or her own, is more than 50 percent likely to have the right answer about some question under consideration, then the group maximizes the chance that it will reach the right answer by insisting on the answer that attracts the most votes. But we have absolutely no right to that assumption when the issues are fundamental moral ones. On the contrary, we all believe that many more people have been wrong about these moral issues, over history and indeed across the world now, than have been right. It would be intolerable hubris to think that Americans are more likely to be right than other human beings have been or are, particularly when Americans are divided so evenly and fiercely as they are now.

Here is a less mathematical but more plausible version of the practical argument for majority rule. We must choose our leaders and our policies by majority vote because we want our leaders to pursue the common good rather than private interests, and which policies are in fact in the common good is a matter of how many people the policies benefit. Whether the common good requires more basketball courts or music halls depends on how many people want one or the other. So the best way to ensure that legislators know where the common good lies, and will work toward it, is to allow the majority in each district to choose the representatives it wants. That is a very popular argument for the efficiency of majoritarian government, and it would be a powerful argument if all political issues were on a par with the choice between basketball courts and music halls. But of course they are not; the questions we have been discussing in this book turn on deep moral issues, not strategies about how to please most people.

So we cannot assume either that majority vote is the uniquely fair way of reaching collective decisions whenever people disagree or that it is always the most accurate or efficient way of making those decisions. But can we say at least this: when a collective political decision must be made and when leaving that decision to chance would seem irrational, then majority rule is the only fair method of decision? We might say: it is uniquely fair then because it allows each person the same influence over the decisions that affect him as anyone else has. That suggestion might make some minimal sense if government were all by town meeting or electronic referendum. But in representative government, people's influence over political decisions is for a thousand reasons never equal; on the contrary, it must be strikingly unequal. At any given moment many thousands of people enjoy elective and appointive office, and the political power of even the lowliest of these will be much greater than most of their fellow citizens who remain in private life. It is no answer to say that all citizens have in the end influence equal to the president's because he, like they, will have only one vote in deciding who wins the next election. That is preposterous; the president and his appointees are given awesome power for several years, and you and I have next to no power to hinder them. Conservatives say that our system of judicial review is undemocratic because the power of five justices trumps that of a majority of the people. But—as Bush's first term showed so dramatically— much of what a single president can do on his own in a single term can never be undone and may be much more consequential, for better or worse, than what all the Supreme Court justices have done together over our whole history.

Representative government is only the most dramatic of the ways in which a very few of us come to have vastly more political power than all the rest even when votes are nominally equal. Political power also very much differs because some of us are much richer than others, or more persuasive in discussion, or have more friends or a larger family, or live in states where the two great political parties are more evenly divided than where others live so that our votes are marginally more likely to make a real difference. These are all familiar reasons why the idea of equal political power is a myth. It is not even an attractive myth because we would not want a Martin Luther King Jr. to have only the political influence that you and I do. Indeed, when we remember how vanishingly *little* political power most of us can have anyway in national or even state political decisions, the question of numerical equality in that infinitesimal quantity of power seems wholly unimportant.

Elsewhere I have suggested a metric for identifying a particular person's political power.[2] Suppose we know nothing about anyone's opinion on some matter of political controversy, and then we learn your opinion and how you will vote when the time for voting comes. By how great an amount does just this information improve the odds—what philosophers call the subjective probability—that your opinion will prevail? If the issue is a national one—whether inheritance taxes are to be reduced, for instance—we would need a great many zeros after the decimal point to express the increased subjective probability. Suppose instead that the issue is whether homosexuality may be criminalized and that issue is to be decided by the Supreme Court. Once again, learning your opinion alone would shift the subjective probabilities because public opinion has some influence on who is appointed to the Court and on how justices decide. Once again, the shift would be infinitesimal, however, and—this is the crucial point—we have no way of knowing in advance whether the shift would be less in the latter case, when the issue is reserved to the courts, than in the former, when it falls to majoritarian politics. The majoritarian conception of democracy, which condemns leaving such issues to the courts, cannot rely on any principle about equal political power to justify its position.

So we must abandon the familiar idea that majority rule is a uniquely fair decision-making procedure, even in politics. In some circumstances, as in the lifeboat and draft cases, it seems highly unfair, and in others, when the question is whether there should be a collective decision on some matter at all, it begs the question. Majority rule is not a particularly sound method of reaching the truth, moreover, and it does not come close to securing equality of political power in a large political community with representative political institutions. We are therefore forced to an important conclusion. The majoritarian conception of democracy is defective because it cannot explain, on its own, what is good about democracy. Mere weight of numbers, on its own, contributes nothing of value to a political decision. We need a deeper and more elaborate account that tells us what conditions must be met and protected in a political community before majority rule is appropriate for that community.

Partnership Democracy: A Rough Sketch

We should return for that purpose to the conception of human dignity that I have been citing and celebrating throughout this book. In the last three chapters I set out my own views about the substantive implications of the two principles of dignity for our policies about human rights, the role of religion in government, and taxation. I offer these opinions as the basis for a contemporary restatement of the liberal position. But of course other Americans who accept these two principles in the abstract will continue to disagree with me and with each other about these implications. So we also need to think about the right procedures for reaching collective decisions when our disagreements persist. We need, that is, to consider not just the substantive but also the procedural implications of the two principles. What structure of political institutions, and of elections to fill those institutions with officials, do those principles recommend?

Equal Concern. Most of us accept this consequence of the first principle of human dignity: a political community must show equal concern for the lives of all those who live within its borders. So we must do our best to ensure that our political officials act with equal concern for all rather than special concern for only some, and that is best achieved with widespread and roughly equal suffrage. Officials elected by a broad swath of the population will do a much better job of protecting the weak against special privilege and tyranny than officials elected by and responsible to only a few. That consequentialist justification for wide suffrage provides no reason, however, for any fetish of mathematical exactness in making people's votes equal in their impact. On the contrary, tinkering and variation may allow for greater representative efficiency and may improve the chances that the final legislative results will better reflect equal concern for all—for example, by consolidating the power of politically isolated minorities. Nor does that justification provide any reason at all for permitting majorities, whenever they wish, to change the basic constitutional structure that seems best calculated to ensure equal concern. We may better protect equal concern by embedding certain individual rights in a constitution that is to be interpreted by judges rather than by elected representatives, and then providing that the constitution can be amended only by supermajorities.

This consequentialist justification of the constitutional structure of the United States does not permit any deep or firm distinction between procedural and substantive fairness. It does not imagine, as supporters of the majoritarian conception do, that there can be any fundamental conflict between the political arrangements that respect equality in the distribution of political power and the legislative policies that respect equality in the distribution of resources and opportunities. On the contrary, this justification supposes that the correct test of whether a political arrangement shows genuine procedural equality is to ask whether that arrangement is likely to produce policies that respect substantive equality in concern for people's lives. But I must now insist on one further principle of great importance that is not captured in that consequentialist justification. We can tinker with districting and other representative arrangements, like filibusters and assigning two senators to each state, large or small, in the hope of perfecting the equal concern that our politics show. But we cannot diminish any citizen's political power by denying him an equal vote for any reason that expresses any measure of contempt for him or any lack of concern for his fate. That would be the most blatant and symbolically outrageous possible violation of the democratic conception of human dignity.

Self-government. Now we must consider this consequence of the second principle of human dignity: political arrangements must respect people's personal responsibility for identifying value in their own lives. I just argued that a majority has no general or automatic right to impose its will on a minority. Under what circumstances does it have that right? In chapter 4 and just now I said that equal concern is a necessary condition of political legitimacy. But it cannot be a sufficient condition, on its own, because people have no moral right to assume coercive authority over others, even when they act in those other people's interest. That would be a flat violation of the second principle of dignity. Democracy is said to be an effective answer to that objection because democracy means *self*-government: it is the form of government in which the people govern themselves. That answer supposes that though it would compromise my dignity to submit myself to the authority of others when I play no part in their decisions, my dignity is not compromised when I do take part, as an equal partner, in those decisions.

That is a crucially important assumption. It explains, if anything can explain, why democratic government is legitimate. It is also the nerve of the partnership conception of democracy; we must ask, in constructing that conception, what rights must be reserved to an individual citizen if submitting to the will of the majority of his fellow citizens in other circumstances is to be consistent with his dignity. The right to participate in political decision, as a voter and as eligible for political office, is obviously essential. So, as we have several times seen, is the equal concern by the majority for his fate. I discussed another crucial condition in chapter 3. It is inconsistent with someone's dignity ever to submit to the coercive authority of others in deciding what role religious or comparable ethical values should play in his life, so the partnership conception requires some guarantee that the majority will not impose its will in these matters. On the partnership conception, therefore, constitutional rights protecting an individual's freedom to make ethical choices for himself are not compromises of democracy but rather attempts to guarantee it.

This brief sketch of the partnership conception fits the basic structure of our own constitutional system very well. It fits that basic structure better than the rival majoritarian conception does because, as I said in distinguishing the two conceptions, our government is not and was not intended to be fully majoritarian. We have representative government, near-universal adult suffrage, and reasonably frequent elections. But we do not insist on mathematical equality of impact in those elections, and some of our legislative institutions, like the Senate and the filibuster, qualify rather than enforce a majoritarian principle. We do insist that no one's vote be denied or compromised for reasons that are inconsistent with recognizing his equal importance and his own responsibility for his life. We embed fundamental freedoms in our Constitution, and we give judges the power to enforce those rights even against a majority's will. In these ways our major institutions provide a framework within which we could construct a full-partnership democracy if we had the political will to do so.

But we do not have a partnership democracy now. In chapter 4 I argued that our laws do not show equal concern for our poor; our failure is so manifest that it compromises our claim to democratic legitimacy. We fall short of a full-partnership democracy in other ways as well: many black and other minority Americans still live as second-class citizens effectively disenfranchised by prejudice and stereotype. The subject of this chapter is not these forms of substantive failure, however. It is the failure of even our electoral procedures, the processes through which we elect our officials, to satisfy the basic requirements of genuine democracy. Public political discourse must have a decent argumentative texture if we are to treat it as an exchange between mutually respectful partners who disagree. Our degraded politics are not only insulting and depressing; they are not even democratic. That is in some ways our most consequential failure because we might hope that we would do better in other ways if our politics were of higher quality.

What Can We Do? First, Education

In previous chapters I tried to illustrate the principles of human dignity I have been exploring through concrete proposals that reflect a liberal interpretation of those principles. In chapter 2 I proposed an approach to the detention of suspected terrorists grounded in a new conception of human rights; in chapter 3 I described how a tolerant secular society would treat its citizens' desire and need for religious expression; in chapter 4 I constructed a model for a redistributive tax program that shows equal concern for all members of the community. I regard these proposals only as illustrations, of course, not as furnishing anything like a complete political program. I shall now offer some further proposals, in the same spirit, to illustrate the distinct procedural claims I have defended in this chapter.

Scholars and other commentators know how bad our politics are, and a great variety of thoughtful proposals have been made for improving them. I mentioned earlier, for example, a book by Ackerman and Fishkin that recommends creating just before each national election a new national holiday called Deliberation Day, during which voters could attend meetings to discuss the election with one another if they wish. We might be skeptical about how many people would wish to spend their new holiday in that way, but every suggestion should be explored. I offer now some more radical proposals, however, which are even less likely to be realized anytime soon but which we would do well to bring into the fringes, at least, of political discussion as soon as possible. When you read these proposals, you might be reminded of the old story about the New England farmer who was asked by strangers how to get to Boston from his farm. "If I were going there," he said, "I wouldn't start from here." But we are here, alas, and we must not abandon hope of getting to a better place.

We should contemplate, among others, three important kinds of change: in education, in the way we run our elections, and in the way we interpret our Constitution. Educational changes would be the most effective and the least disruptive to tradition if we could only achieve them. The difficulties, however, are famously great. Just before the 2004 election, a medical technician saw a copy of *The New York Review of Books* on my table and said he assumed that meant I would vote for Kerry. He would not, he said, and he explained why. He knew the issues were complex; he knew that many educated people thought that the treatment of our prisoners in Guantánamo and elsewhere was unjust, for example, and also thought that Bush's tax reductions were economically very unwise. But he knew that other people who also thought themselves experts disagreed with all those judgments, and he was wholly without the ability to judge these matters for himself. So he would vote for Bush because he was religious and knew that Bush was religious too. What else, he asked me, could he do?

We must no longer tolerate secondary school education that puts so many thoughtful voters in that impossible and undemocratic position. The most daunting but also most urgent requirement is to make a Contemporary Politics course part of every high school curriculum. I do not mean civics lessons in which students are taught the structure of our government or history courses in which America's story is celebrated. I mean courses that take up issues that are among the most contentious political controversies of the day: issues like those discussed in this book. The dominant pedagogical aim must be to instill some sense of the complexity of these issues, some understanding of positions different from those the students are likely to find at home or among friends, and some idea of what a conscientious and respectful argument over these issues might be like. The dominant pedagogical strategy should be an attempt to locate these controversies in different interpretations of principles the students might be expected themselves to accept: for example, the two principles of human dignity that I believe are common ground in America now. The courses might well include a suitably simplified examination of classics of Western political philosophy from both the conservative and liberal traditions: some understanding of the ideas of Aquinas, Locke, Kant, Rawls, and Hayek, for example, mainly through secondary sources if necessary. The materials and teaching must be geared to the abilities of high school students, of course, but I believe that we are more likely to underestimate than overestimate those abilities. People who can master the intricacies of peer-to-peer file sharing through the Internet should have no trouble with the Categorical Imperative; indeed some study of the latter might help them in deciding whether the former is fair.

Contemporary Politics courses would be extremely challenging and difficult to teach, particularly before some broad consensus had developed among teachers and in schools about how they should be taught. Teachers would have to steer between anodyne banality and indoctrination, and they would have to recognize that the first of these failures is as much to be avoided as the second. But think how much it would improve our politics if students leaving high school had some understanding of the reasons why a deeply devout person might nevertheless prefer a tolerant secular to a tolerant religious state or why an atheist might think that public celebrations of religion were appropriate in a nation the vast majority of whose members were religious. Or if those students had asked themselves whether their nation had an obligation of equal concern to all its citizens and what, if any, were the implications of that obligation for redistributive taxation and social welfare programs. Or if they had been asked to consider what differences were morally permissible in a state's treatment of citizens and aliens. Or if they had actually read and debated the opinion of Justice Marshall in the Massachusetts gay marriage case and, if they disagreed with her judgment, they had been challenged to say why. Or if they had been invited to consider what made a theory scientific and whether the "intelligent design" theory of creation met whatever standard for classification as science they considered appropriate.

I know, of course, that this suggestion bristles with possibly insuperable political difficulties. The selection of texts would be intensely controversial, and the danger of manipulation by local political and religious groups very great indeed. It would be much easier for everyone—school boards, school principals, and teachers in particular—if nothing like this were attempted. But that would nevertheless be shaming. We cheat our children inexcusably if we allow the nation to continue only to masquerade as democratic. The idea that public education is school for democracy is certainly not new; it was at the center of John Dewey's enormously influential educational philosophy. What is new in this suggestion is only content and ambition, and that is driven only by a more realistic opinion of what genuine democracy needs and the cost we pay in legitimacy so long as we fail to provide it.

Elections

We must also change how we elect our leaders. Election law—the regulation of political financing, campaigns, representation, and voting procedures—is an elaborate and growing branch of legal theory. I shall suggest, by way of illustration only, some radical directions that that law might now take. I have not tried to elaborate my proposals in any detail or to consider either the practical or the political obstacles to implementing them. Most of those obstacles are obvious enough. Nor have I tried to confront certain evident problems of detail that each proposal raises, including the treatment of third- or minor-party candidates. I set these proposals out in this rough form mainly to consider whether the natural objections they inevitably attract are plausible. Mental blocks are among the most powerful obstacles to new directions. Consider then the follow illustrative proposals.

Public Election Channels. Congress should create and fund two special public broadcasting channels to offer continuous election coverage during each presidential election period. These networks should be subject to severe equal-time and fairness coverage restrictions but should be otherwise free to develop their own news programs, bulletins, talk shows, and analyses. Presidential candidates would be required to hold regularly scheduled press conferences that are broadcast and organized by these public networks, and extensive follow-up questioning would be permitted at these news conferences. Election debates would be organized by and broadcast on these public networks, and the rules of those debates would be established by legislation not subject to variation by candidate agreement. A bipartisan election channel commission with deans of prominent journalism schools as ex-officio members would appoint the officers of these networks and have broad powers to supervise fairness and equal-time standards.

Regulation of Private Networks and Affiliates. Overall television and radio expenditure by or on behalf of any candidate should be strictly limited without regard to the source of his funds. Political commercials in the familiar form should be forbidden on all networks except subject to the following regulations: the advertisement must run for a minimum of three minutes, of which at least two minutes must consist in a candidate for office or an officer of an organization that has paid for the advertisement speaking directly to the camera.

Right of Comment. During a presidential election period, each of the major terrestrial and cable networks should be required to set aside a prime-time slot of half an hour each week, to be made available to each of the major parties to correct what it takes to be errors or bias in that network's reporting and political opinion broadcasts during the preceding week. The parties would be required to submit advance tapes of the proposed material, and though the network would be required to broadcast the material as presented, it would be permitted to prepare a rebuttal if it wished.

Lawyers will tell you that these suggestions have one thing in common: they are all unconstitutional because they are violations of our Constitution's First Amendment guarantees of freedom of speech. I would contest that, as a legal opinion, at least as to some of these sample suggestions. I believe that some of the Supreme Court's decisions applying First Amendment principles to election law, including its well-known and much regretted decision holding that limits on campaign expenditure are unconstitutional, were wrong when decided and remain wrong.[3] But my immediate concern is not with constitutional law but with political principle. Free speech is not just a clause in our constitutional document; it is an important human right now recognized in similar national and international documents around the world. Would the moral and political principles behind the First Amendment, the principles that justify giving that particular freedom that constitutional status, be outraged by regulations of election speech of the kind I am imagining?

We must now ask the question about the right of free speech that I asked in chapter 3 about the companion right of religious freedom. What more basic principles or policies justify protecting speech in that special way? There is an extensive literature among constitutional scholars and political philosophers devoted to that question, and much of it makes the important point that there is no single answer. Freedom of speech serves a considerable variety of important principles and policies. But two of these are most in point in our discussion now. First, freedom of speech is a crucial part of the rights people must have to protect their personal responsibility under the second principle of human dignity: the responsibility to identify and seek value in their own lives. Second, that freedom is a crucially important condition for the realization of any plausible conception of democracy: it is plainly essential to the partnership conception that I said we should favor. We must therefore ask whether the radical changes in election law that I propose would compromise either of these fundamental reasons for protecting speech.

Preventing someone from speaking his conscience and conviction to other people is a particularly grave harm. People develop their ethical and moral personalities most effectively in conversation and exchange with others. Speaking out for what one believes—bearing witness and testimony—is in any case for most people an essential part of believing; it is part of the total phenomenon of conviction. Identifying oneself to others as a person of particular beliefs or faiths is part of creating one's identity, part of the process of self-creation that is at the center of our personal responsibility. Silencing someone's political speech is a particularly devastating insult because it denies his role as a full partner in self-government. So we should be particularly attentive to the danger of regulating political speech in any way.

But we should not be bewitched by that danger; we should look more closely at the effects of the particular regulation that is proposed. There is no risk to a political candidate's personality or to his success in identifying his convictions to others in requiring him to speak for himself on television during the election period rather than through an actor and to describe and defend his convictions rather than simply smiling through jingles. These constraints in no way compromise his authenticity or sincerity; they can only improve those qualities by making distortion and evasion more difficult. There is no threat to the ethical or moral integrity of a network's chief executive officer or to any of its corporate owners or shareholders when the network is required to broadcast comments on its election coverage plainly labeled as representing the opinions of others not its own. These regulations may be costly.

The money that networks would lose by forgoing political commercials and by sacrificing prime-time slots for political rebuttals would be considerable, and a public subsidy to cover these costs might be appropriate. But that is another matter, and it has nothing to do with freedom of speech. We do not think that anyone's integrity of personality is threatened by laws forbidding cigarette or liquor advertising on television or by requiring advertisements for medicine to be vetted for accuracy. The damage that our politics now does to democracy is as grave as the damage to health carried by that forbidden advertising.

The second reason for protecting freedom of speech that I mentioned is equally important. People do not govern themselves if they are deprived of the information they need to make intelligent decisions or cheated of the criticism they need in order effectively to judge the record of their officials. But the regulations I propose have no such consequence. On the contrary, they are designed to improve the public's chances of receiving the information it requires in a form that is more helpful because it is less distorted and obfuscated. It is true that many people would find the kind of television politics the proposed regulations would create less to their tastes. They might well prefer mindless personal attacks set to catchy political tunes to a three-minute argument about political economy. If we were drawn to the majoritarian conception of democracy, we might count that a serious objection. We might think that people are entitled to as much choice as possible in how they wanted their politics presented. But on the partnership conception, too much is at stake for that. If the fairness of an election depends on the character of the argument that precedes the vote, then people have no democratic right that their politics be wrapped in entertainment.

Constitutional Law and the Commander in Chief

This chapter has been about the procedures of democracy: I have argued that we must reject the familiar majoritarian understanding of democracy. Majoritarianism seems appealing because it separates procedure from substance, focusing on how people who disagree about substance can nevertheless agree how fairly to resolve their differences. But that apparent advantage disappears once we realize that majority rule has no independent virtues of fairness, that its claims to fairness arise only when certain substantive conditions have already been identified and satisfied. Philosophers have long wanted a purely procedural account of political fairness, but there is none to be had.

So I have been talking about democracy in this book all along. The basic ethical principles of human dignity that I described in chapter 1 are the source of democratic values. The freedom I identified in our discussion of church and state in chapter 3 must be protected if we are to have democracy. So must the equal concern that I discussed in chapter 4. I agree that it would be neater firmly to separate these substantive issues from procedural questions about democracy, but political values are finally unitary, not plural. Earlier in this chapter I imagined a response to the preceding chapters: that my criticisms might be answered by pointing out that the American people apparently approve, even if only just barely, of how our government is governing. But that, as we have now discovered, is a wholly futile response, for if the Bush administration's programs are wrong in the way I charge, popular consent cannot cure them.

Throughout the book my focus has been on political principle rather than on constitutional or international law. But I shall end by saying something about our Constitution because it is one of America's greatest political advantages, an advantage that a great many other nations are now doing their best to secure for themselves. The Constitution not only protects individual rights but does so in highly abstract terms that allow lawyers and laymen to conduct a continuing argument about how best to interpret its principles. We have encountered the Constitution's abstract vocabulary in each chapter: I have mentioned due process and the equal protection of the laws, freedom of speech, the free exercise of religion, the prohibition on any establishment of religion. For better or for worse, these now runic phrases have built theaters for legal theory and political philosophy. The protection they offer is far from perfect; the runic language is after all antique and was not deployed with contemporary problems in mind. The Supreme Court has the last word, for practical purposes, about how the language should be interpreted, and its record is stained with serious error at almost every period of its jurisprudence. We all worry, red and blue alike, about the direction the Court will take in the future, and though it is worth noticing that most of the past decisions we now most regret were decisions in which the Court refused to overturn unlawful executive or legislative decisions, we must concede that it has also made mistakes in the opposite direction, overruling other branches of government when it should not have done so.

Still, the Constitution gives us an opportunity for a kind and dimension of public argument that we would otherwise lack. It allows us to conduct an important part of the argument I said we need in the disciplined language of legal and hence political principle. Several of the issues I have been discussing in this book have been argued in that way—courtrooms have been the prime forums for such debate as we have had about religion in our politics and public life, for instance—not just among professional lawyers but also to the public at large in newspapers and popular journals. We have only just begun a constitutional legal debate about the issues I raised in chapter 2, about whether and how far, in our attempts to defend ourselves against further terrorist attacks, we may abandon the protections of individuals that we have thought essential to human dignity. That may prove, however, to be among the most important debates we have ever had. The Bush administration claims unprecedented authority to act free of a variety of legal constraints when it deems this necessary in our defense. It has claimed the power to torture its prisoners, and to order their "rendition" to other countries that will torture them, in spite of laws flatly forbidding torture. It has claimed the power secretly to tap telephone calls not just between foreigners but between Americans as well—with no judicial warrant or congressional oversight of any kind—whenever the president or his agents determine that security so requires. The president says that he may put himself above the law in that way because the Constitution declares that the president is commander in chief, and so no other branch of government has the constitutional right to limit or question his authority in wartime. That is a particularly frightening claim when we remember that the "war" in question will probably continue, if it ever ends, for decades. Only one institution—the Court—has the practical power to check this serious threat to American values and freedom.

You may be surprised that I have retained my enthusiasm for trusting important matters of political morality to constitutional judges. Time was when most of my colleagues in American law schools shared that enthusiasm, but they belong mainly to the blue culture, and their admiration was fueled by the Supreme Court's steady and improving protection of individual freedom in the decades after the Second World War. Their faith in the Court has now been dampened by a cold rain of right-wing activism in the other direction. The very conservative Justices Antonin Scalia and Clarence Thomas have now been joined on the Court by Bush's new appointees—Chief Justice John Roberts and Justice Samuel Alito—who are widely thought to share the convictions and agenda of those justices. There are worrying signs that the Supreme Court, now likely to be dominated by conservatives for at least another generation, will set out not only to repeal those advances in individual rights but to achieve what can only be regarded as a revolutionary change in the balance of power among institutions of government: transferring power from Congress to state legislatures and ratifying instead of denying the claims of the Bush administration to unprecedented sovereign authority.

I would regret this anticipated—though hardly inevitable—shift of the Supreme Court sharply to the right. But if we believe that the majoritarian conception of democracy is unsatisfactory and that we must embrace a partnership conception instead, then we must remember the contribution that a judicial institution with the Supreme Court's powers can make to that latter ideal. We must not condemn judicial review as undemocratic whenever we disagree with the decisions the Court makes. I am worried, however, about an ideological administration appointing young ideological justices whose tenure on the Court will last for generations, long after the nation has steered itself back to the middle as, so far, it always has. Judicial appointments have become more political, and presidents use them strategically to play to particular constituencies. Presidents also take greater care not to be surprised in the way presidents once were. Dwight Eisenhower said that he had made two major mistakes in his administration and that they were both on the Supreme Court. He meant Chief Justice Earl Warren and Justice William Brennan, who became very liberal justices once on the Court. Presidents are much more careful now, and such mistakes are less likely, though of course not impossible.

I would recommend this change: we should amend the Constitution to institute a term limit for Supreme Court justices, a maximum of fifteen years' tenure, perhaps. I know that some of our greatest judges served much longer terms than that, and I understand that in adjudication, as in many things, experience counts and practice may make perfect. I also understand that scheduled retirements would allow litigants to make strategic decisions about when to institute a case that may come before the Court. Still, I think the dangers of ideological judges serving for many decades are too great to continue to run the risk. If we did establish a term limit for Supreme Court justices, the limit would of course have to apply only to justices appointed after the change. And we would have to think of what to do with ex-justices, some of whom would be much too young to retire to write their memoirs. They could not be allowed to take up corporate appointments or law firm partnerships or to run for public office; the risk of an appearance of corruption while on the bench would be too great. But they could be appointed to lower courts, and they could, if the indignity were not too great, take up teaching in law schools, where the only possible corruption would be a benign penchant for praising their own opinions.

EPILOGUE

I SAID THAT I wanted to start an argument, and I've done my best. I hope that whether you belong to the red nation or the blue, you have found something in what I've said to argue about and not only to cheer or hate. I set out, in the beginning, two basic principles of human dignity that I can now restate with certain refinements I added later. These principles hold, first, that each human life is intrinsically and equally valuable and, second, that each person has an inalienable personal responsibility for identifying and realizing value in his or her own life. I argued that almost all Americans—and almost all citizens of other nations with similar political cultures—can embrace these two principles, indeed that they could not consistently reject either without abandoning ethical or religious commitments they cherish. I claimed that these principles can serve as common ground on which Americans who are now very deeply divided about politics can construct what we now, to our shame, lack: a real political argument.

Abstract principles are useless without concrete illustrations; I tried to defend my claims by showing how these two principles bear on four issues of particularly heated political controversy now: human rights and terrorism, religion in our public life, taxation and the redistribution of economic resources, and the character and procedures of democracy. In a few years we may be locked into very different controversies. We may have stopped talking about Hurricane Katrina, the alternative minimum tax, and gay marriage and begun to occupy ourselves more seriously with genetic engineering, global warming, or our responsibilities to desperately poor people in far-away countries. But the two basic dimensions of dignity will remain, and they will still command our respect. The principles are not in themselves political, but they have striking political implications because anyone who accepts them must also accept that a government compromises its legitimacy when it does not provide equal concern for everyone over whom it claims dominion or does not protect the rights that people need in order to exercise personal responsibility for their own lives.

I relied on these dimensions of dignity to argue for political positions that I believe form the best understanding of liberalism now. I suggested, among other claims, that any adequate theory of human rights insists that a nation not injure anyone in the way its laws and traditions forbid it to injure its own citizens; that only a tolerant secular state respects the personal responsibility of its citizens for ethical value; that a legitimate state must aim at ex ante equality through a tax structure inspired by the old political ideal of a collective insurance pool; and that democracy requires a culture of political argument and respect, not just naked majority rule. At each stage of this argument I challenged those who disagree with the liberalism I defend—either from the Left or from the Right—to construct an argument toward different conclusions, beginning in different interpretations of the two principles.

I did my best to suggest the direction that these contrary arguments might take. Many people believe that relaxing our concern for personal privacy, civil liberties, and legal safeguards is not unfair but only a sensible response to genuine, terrible threats to our safety; that a new emphasis on religion in our politics and government is only fair, given that most Americans believe in God and want that emphasis; that fairness as well as efficiency demands a tax policy that rewards achievement; and that Americans are entitled to the kind of politics they find most congenial even if the few intellectuals who talk about deliberative democracy would prefer a more cerebral brand. I propose that we debate which of these radically different sets of political positions—the liberal principles I set out or these more conservative alternatives—better captures and expresses the deeper values locked into the two principles of dignity. I have set out my side of that argument. Those who disagree can and I hope will construct stronger counterarguments than I have managed.

Some people who do take up that challenge might prefer a different strategy, however. If they discover or come to suspect that the political positions they favor actually do contradict one or the other of those two principles, they might then prefer to reject the principles rather than to change their politics. That is not always an impermissible strategy. We often test principles by speculating about their consequences in practice and then rejecting the principles if we cannot abide those consequences. The strategy would be fatal in this case, however, because the principles I describe are for most of us such deep premises of our entire structures of value that we could not in fact abandon them. We could only tell ourselves that we have and then lead deeply inauthentic lives. We cannot give up the idea that it is really important how we live our lives or that how we live is finally our own responsibility.

Other readers might be tempted to dispose of the challenge in a different way: by ignoring it altogether. Many people have no interest in philosophical challenges to their settled political preferences. They do not wish to ask themselves whether they can square those preferences with principles about life and dignity that they would be uncomfortable rejecting. They treat their politics as a matter of flat allegiance, not reasoned decision, as fans treat baseball teams. They delight in cartoons of a simian President Bush dragging his hands on the ground or in books with titles like *How to Talk to a Liberal (If You Must)*.[1] Real argument or introspection is the last thing they have in mind. They achieve

this state of mind through a rigid intellectual compartmentalization: they lock their personal ideals of value and dignity in a separate chamber of their personalities that is well insulated from their
politics. They can embrace fully humane ideas about the importance of human life and then vote for politicians who promise to
cut social welfare programs; they can insist on their own personal
responsibility for religious faith and then applaud politicians who
promise to create a Christian country.

This insulation is morally irresponsible. For almost all of us,
politics is the chief moral theater of our lives. The choices we
make together in voting and lobbying are enormously consequential, and it is shabby not to confront those choices demanding of
ourselves full personal integrity. In chapter 1 I said that we show
contempt for ourselves when we have inadequate concern for the
dignity of others—for the importance of their lives and their responsibility for those lives. We compound that self-contempt when
we work to make ourselves unaware of it; compartmentalization is
not only a serious moral failure but a grave failure in personal dignity as well. This book's premise is that enough Americans value
their self-respect to make a difference.

Is it possible to bring genuine democracy to America? I've offered many reasons for supposing not, and you may think that the
great political improbability of many of the changes I've suggested
only reinforces my apparent pessimism. But I should tell you as I
close that I myself retain a perhaps perverse optimism because
there is so much good and wise in our country. We are now, I
think, in a particularly depressing and dangerous period of our
history. But if you take a longer perspective, you may share some
of my hope. Americans of goodwill, intelligence, and ambition
have given the world, over the last two centuries, much of what is
best in it now.

We gave the world the idea of a constitution protecting the
rights of minorities, including religious dissenters and atheists, a
constitution that has been the envy of other nations and is now in-
creasingly, at least indirectly, an inspiration for them. We gave the
world a lesson in national generosity after the Second World War,

and we gave it leadership then in its new enthusiasm for international organization and international law. We gave it the idea, striking in mid-twentieth-century Europe, that social justice is not the preserve of socialism; we gave it the idea of an egalitarian capitalism and, in the New Deal, a serious if limited step toward that achievement. These are the very ideas and ideals that many people in the rest of the world think we have now abandoned. But the roots of the love of dignity in our national character that allowed us to lead in these ways cannot entirely have withered. I called for argument in this book, and you may think that I have now, at the very end, fallen back only on faith. You may be right. But argument is pointless without faith in those with whom you argue.

NOTES

Chapter 1   Common Ground

1. See my article in "The Election and America's Future," *The New York Review of Books*, November 4, 2004.

2. Newt Gingrich, *Winning the Future* (Regnery, 2005), xiv.

3. Throughout this book, unless the context dictates otherwise, I use masculine pronouns as gender-neutral references.

4. I elaborate this conception of the relation between liberty and equality in my books *Sovereign Virtue* (Harvard University Press, 2000) and *Justice in Robes* (Harvard University Press, 2006), chapter 4.

5. I describe these phenomena at greater length in my book *Life's Dominion* (Knopf, 1993).

6. See my article "You'd Better Believe It," *Philosophy & Public Affairs* (1991).

7. Robert P. George, *Making Men Moral: Civil Liberties and Public Morality* (Oxford University Press, 1993), 106. George describes a paternalist I once imagined, who thinks that people's lives go better if they are forced to pray, as a "straw man." "It is hard to imagine a God foolish enough to be tricked by or pleased by such imitation prayer or a modern person foolish enough to believe in such a God."

Chapter 2   Terrorism and Human Rights

1. For a statement of the case against the president's claim, see the letter to members of Congress on National Security Agency spying from

fourteen former officials and constitutional scholars, *The New York Review of Books*, February 9, 2006.

2. See my article "What the Court Really Said," *The New York Review of Books*, August 12, 2004.

3. *Hamdan v. Rumsfeld*, 415 F.3d 33 (2005).

4. That is my own view. See *Sovereign Virtue*, chapters 11 and 12.

5. See my book *Justice for Hedgehogs* (Harvard University Press, forthcoming).

Chapter 3   Religion and Dignity

1. See *Bob Jones III Retiring from University*, http://www.msnbc.msn.com/id/6850482/from/RL.5/.

2. See Joseph Loconte, "Isaiah Was a Democrat," *International Herald Tribune*, January 3, 2006.

3. See "How Family's Cause Reached the Halls of Congress," *New York Times*, March 22, 2005, section A, p. 1.

4. See John Danforth, "In the Name of Politics," *New York Times*, March 30, 2005, section A, p. 17.

5. *New York Times*, November 4, 2004, section A, p. 25.

6. *Lynch v. Donnelly*, 465 U.S. 668 (1984).

7. See the dissenting opinion of Justice Potter Stewart in *Abington School District v. Schempp*, 374. U.S. 2003 (1963).

8. *United States v. Macintosh*, 283 U.S. 605 (1931). Gingrich, *Winning the Future*, ix, 69.

9. *Zorach v. Clauson*, 343 U.S. 306 (1952).

10. *Engel v. Vitale* 370 U.S. 421 (1962).

11. *Allegheny County v. ACLU*, 492 U.S. 573 (1989), Justice Kennedy dissenting.

12. See my discussion of Rawls's idea of public reason in *Justice in Robes*, chapter 9.

13. John Rawls, *Collected Papers* (Harvard University Press, 1997), 588–89.

14. Gingrich, *Winning the Future*, xxi.

15. My formulation runs against the grain of much contemporary political philosophy because it merges different values that philosophers like to keep distinct; it makes the scope of liberty depend on other values, including those of distributive justice. See the discussion of democracy in chapter 5. I defend my view that political values cannot be understood independently of one another in *Justice in Robes*, chapter 6, and, at a more philosophical level, in *Justice for Hedgehogs*.

16. *United States v. Seegar*, 380 U.S. 163, 166 (1965).

17. *Planned Parenthood of Pennsylvania v. Casey*, 505 US 833 (1992).

18. *Lawrence v. Texas*, 539 U.S. 558 (2003).

19. Gingrich, *Winning the Future*, ix, 69.

20. Dworkin, *Life's Dominion*.

21. See Denise Grady, "Study Finds 29-Week Fetuses Probably Feel No Pain and Need No Abortion Anesthesia," *New York Times*, August 24, 2005, section A, p. 10.

22. I discuss the question of the interests of people dead or unconscious in *Life's Dominion*.

23. *Kitzmiller et al. v. Dover Area School Board*, Federal District Court Middle Area Pennsylvania, Judge John Jones Memorandum Opinion, December 20, 2005.

24. Elisabeth Bumiller, "Bush Remarks Roil Debate over Teaching of Evolution," *New York Times*, August 3, 2005, section A, p. 14.

25. David Stout, "Frist Urges 2 Teachings on Life Origin," *New York Times*, August 20, 2005, section A, p. 10.

26. See *Kitzmiller et al. v. Dover Area School Board*. For a very clear statement of the scientific errors in the intelligent design argument, see Philip M. Boffey, "The Evolution Wars, Revisited," *New York Times on the Web*, http://select.nytimes.com/2006/01/18/opinion/18talkingpoints .html?pagewanted=all8dpc.

27. Bumiller, "Bush Remarks Roil."

Chapter 4 Taxes and Legitimacy

1. See Michael A. Fletcher and Jonathan Weisman, "Bush Renews Push for Extending Tax Cuts," *Washington Post*, December 6, 2005, p. A02.

2. Arthur B. Kennickell, "A Rolling Tide: Changes in the Distribution of Wealth in the U.S., 1989–2001," table 10 (Levy Economics Institute, November 2003).

3. http://www.census.gov/hhes/income/histinc/ie3.html.

4. See "A Marie Antoinette Moment," *International Herald Tribune*, January 3, 2006, p. 6.

5. See Joel Friedman and Robert Greenstein, "Exempting Corporate Dividends from Individual Income Taxes," Center for Budget and Policy Priorities, January 6, 2003.

6. See "Wanted: A Wary Audience," *New York Times*, January 31, 2006, section A, p. 20.

7. See "Economy Up, People Down: Declining Earnings Undercut Income Growth," Economic Policy Institute Publication, http://www.epi .org/content.cfm/webfeatures_econindicators_income20050831.

8. See "Average American Family Income Declines," http://abcnews
.go.com/Business/wireStory?id=1654810&business=true.

9. See Council of Economic Advisers, "Strengthening America's Economy: The President's Jobs and Growth Proposals," January 7, 2003.

10. "Wanted: A Wary Audience."

11. Joseph Stiglitz, "Bush's Tax Plan—the Dangers," *The New York
Review of Books*, March 13, 2003.

12. See, e.g., Thomas Frank, *What's the Matter with Kansas* (Henry
Holt, 2004).

13. See, e.g., Ian Shapiro, *The State of Democratic Theory* (Princeton
University Press, 2003).

14. See the discussion of Rawls in chapter 3 and in *Justice in Robes*,
chapter 9.

15. That claim is forcefully argued in Liam Murphy and Thomas
Nagel, *The Myth of Ownership: Taxes and Justice* (Oxford University
Press, 2002).

16. See Dworkin, *Sovereign Virtue*, chapters 2 and 3.

17. Ibid., chapter 2.

18. See the discussion ibid., chapters 8 and 9.

19. We cannot rule out the possibility that some very few people
would not have insured themselves at least to that level. But we do not
know which people would not have done so, if indeed any would not,
and if the probability is overwhelming that any particular person would
have insured at that level, fairness requires us to treat everyone on the
assumption that he would have done so.

20. This is a structure, more precisely, for reflecting on what fairness
requires in a tax system. Taxes pay for public goods that are not redistributive, and they also serve fiscal policy as well as social justice. The
timing of tax reductions and increases must take account of whether the
economy as a whole needs stimulation or dampening. Allowing government that leeway for timing is in the interests of everyone, including
those at the bottom. But even when fiscal policy argues for reducing
taxes, distributive questions remain, and it is not only fair but also efficient that the share of the burden borne by rich taxpayers should then
increase, not decrease, as it has under the Bush administration. In fact,
whatever fiscal benefit has come from that administration's tax cuts has
come from the moderate tax reductions on the middle class and poor,
not from the much more dramatic reductions for the rich.

21. See Murphy and Nagel, *Myth of Ownership*. See also Justine Bur-
ley, ed., *Dworkin and His Critics* (Blackwells, 2004), 353.

22. See *Sovereign Virtue*, especially chapters 2 and 9.

23. See, e.g., Jeff Madrick, "Health for Sale," *The New York Review of Books*, December 18, 2003: "Claims made by well-known economists such as Martin Feldstein, former chairman of President Reagan's Council of Economic Advisers, that high taxes discourage people from working hard and investing more have not held up. Clinton's tax increases in 1992, which Feldstein and others warned would reduce incentives to work and invest, helped or at the least did not impede the economic boom of the late 1990s." For a similar view from an avowedly right-wing commentator, see Bruce Bartlett, "What Bush Boom?" http://economists view.typepad.com/economistsview/2006/03/what_bush_boom.html.

24. However, there is some evidence that corporations prefer higher taxes and a workforce that is better educated through the educational system that higher taxes make possible. See Paul Krugman's account of Toyota's decision to build a new plant in Ontario rather than in the American South, "Toyota, Moving North," *New York Times*, July 25, 2005, section A, p. 19.

25. See Murphy and Nagel, *Myth of Ownership*. See also my article "Do Liberty and Equality Conflict," in Paul Barker, ed., *Living as Equals* (Oxford University Press, 1996).

Chapter 5   Is Democracy Possible?

1. Bruce Ackerman and James Fishkin, *Deliberation Day* (Yale University Press, 2004).

2. See Dworkin, *Sovereign Virtue*, chapter 4.

3. The campaign finance decision is *Buckley v. Vallejo*, 424 U.S. 1 (1974). For my argument that that decision was wrong, see *Sovereign Virtue*, chapter 10.

Epilogue

1. Ann Coulter, *How to Talk to a Liberal (If You Must)* (Crown Forum, 2004).

INDEX